multiCultural folktales

stories to tell young children

judy sierra &
robert Kaminski

oryx

The rare Arabian Oryx is believed to have inspired the myth of the unicorn. This desert antelope became virtually extinct in the early 1960s. At that time several groups of international conservationists arranged to have 9 animals sent to the Phoenix Zoo to be the nucleus of a captive breeding herd. Today the Oryx population is nearly 800, and over 400 have been returned to reserves in the Middle East.

Published by The Oryx Press
4041 North Central at Indian School Road
Phoenix, Arizona 85012-3397

Published simultaneously in Canada

Printed and Bound in the United States of America

⊗ The paper used in this publication meets the minimum requirements of American National Standard for Information Science—Permanence of Paper for Printed Library Materials, ANSI Z39.48, 1984.

Library of Congress Cataloging-in-Publication Data

Sierra, Judy
   Multicultural folktales: stories to tell young children / Judy Sierra & Robert Kaminski.
      p.   cm.
   Includes bibliographical references and index.
   ISBN 0-89774-688-0
   1. Tales.   2. Puppet theater in education.   3. Flannelgraphs.
4. Storytelling.   I. Kaminski, Robert.   II. Title.
GR69.S54   1991
398.2--dc20   91-29533
                                                        CIP

In order to keep this title in print and available to the academic community, this edition was produced using digital reprint technology in a relatively short print run. This would not have been attainable using traditional methods. Although the cover has been changed from its original appearance, the text remains the same and all materials and methods used still conform to the highest book-making standards.

Contents

Acknowledgments

Thanks to Linda White of the Santa Cruz Public Library for sharing her creative techniques of making flannel board figures from felt and paper, and also the staff and children of Bayview Elementary School, Santa Cruz, California, for listening and joining in.

Introduction

Folktales come to us through the oral tradition, so it is quite natural that we look to this source for stories to tell aloud to children. The type of folktales that are appropriate for young children have a clear and obvious structure. Often, for example, episodes are repeated three or more times with only minor variations. The use of language in folktales is often poetic. Many of these traditional tales include rhythmic or rhyming refrains that are easy to learn and enjoyable to say together as a group. Characters are memorable for their unusual names and highly exaggerated (even stereotyped) traits—the cruel ogre, the tricky fox, the greedy rich man. Oral traits which have enabled folktales to survive for centuries without being written down make these stories easy for the beginning storyteller to learn and perform. The plot, characters, and structure of an unfamiliar tale will very often resemble those of tales the storyteller already knows.

No matter how nonsensical or outlandish a folktale may seem at first hearing, most that have managed to remain favorites in oral and written tradition contain important commentaries on social relationships and behavior. For example, cumulative animal tales such as "The Cat and the Mouse," and "The Elegant Rooster" contain seemingly endless repetition, which children find hilariously funny. This repetition encourages children to develop their memories as they join in repeating ever-lengthening refrains. But in addition, these two tales embody basic lessons about exchange between the members of human society—the first story, the exchange of valuable objects, the second, the exchange of favors. The best tales serve several functions, and are open to multiple interpretations. As a result, the teller can share them again and again, never exhausting the possibility of finding—and giving—new meaning to them.

A country or area of origin is given for each folktale in this book, though this merely indicates the place in which one particular version of the story was collected. Very similar stories may exist in the oral and literary traditions of many geographical areas. Folklore researchers refer to a group of stories with similar core plot and characters as a **tale type**, and to a particular tale that has this basic core as a **variant** of the tale type. For example, the tale, "The Goat in the Chile Patch," is a New Mexican variant of Tale Type 2015, *The Goat Who Would Not Go Home*.[1] Other variants of this tale type are known throughout Europe and the Americas—although how, when, and why these similar tales developed or spread is not known.

The importance of tale types for those of us who work with young children is that there may be several variants of one tale type published in picture book editions and in anthologies. These provide children five and older with a perfect introduction to comparative literature. They are quite delighted to recognize similarities in tales, and to enumerate their differences. Knowing how to locate variants also gives us a choice of tellings—we can find the one that best suits our taste. See "Resources for Storytelling," at the end of this book, for help in locating tale variants.

Although the study of folktales has a place in the social studies curriculum, it would be unwise to draw hasty or generalized conclusions about a culture or a country on the basis of its folktales—and particularly not on the basis of the select few that

---

[1]Aarne, Antti and Stith Thompson. *The Types of the Folktale: A Classification and Bibliography*. Folklore Fellows Communications, no. 184. Helsinki: Suomalainen Tiedeakatemia, 1973.

have made their way into North American children's literature. Folktales often portray a way of life that is centuries old, or that is pure fantasy. However, we do like to let our listeners know the source of the tales we tell them, and we stress that people everywhere enjoy stories and that the fact that we can appreciate one anothers' stories shows how much we are alike. As we enjoy another culture's stories, we extend our knowledge and sensitivity of the global community. By studying a culture, we can discover which aspects of its folktales are indeed part of the life of that group, and also select other culturally relevant details to add to our retellings. Three of the stories in this book, "The Elegant Rooster," "The Goat in the Chile Patch," and "La Hormiguita," are presented in both English and Spanish.

The 25 stories and rhymes in this book are arranged in youngest-to-oldest order, with those at the beginning most suitable for children two-and-a-half to five, those in the latter part of the book for children five to seven. The first 13 stories are accompanied by patterns for flannel board figures, because we have found that preschool children in groups need to focus their attention visually during the telling of stories. Most classrooms and libraries are visually stimulating environments (and rightly so), and have noise distractions as well. Through the use of puppets and flannel boards, storytellers can better keep children's attention and help them develop their ability to concentrate. It is also easier to tell stories to young children if they can participate verbally and physically in the storytelling. Participation ideas and techniques for encouraging and controlling participation are suggested in the storytelling instructions which accompany each tale.

PART 1
Storytelling Techniques and Materials

Storytelling

CHOOSING AND LEARNING A STORY TO TELL

Always select stories that you like. Children must like them too, of course, so read the stories you select aloud to a child or a group of children of the appropriate age, and observe their response. Young children may not be able to put their response into words, but quiet attention is a sign of interest, as are questions afterward and requests to hear the story again. Successful stories are those that please both the teller and the audience.

The shortest stories are not necessarily the easiest to learn. Ones with much repetition of scenes, phrases, and refrains, or that resemble other stories the teller already knows are good choices for the beginner. The flannel board serves as a memory aid for the storyteller as well as a visual aid for the audience. Rhythmic, cumulative tales such as "La Hormiguita" and "The Elegant Rooster" work well with audiences of very young children, and with children who are learning English. For mixed-age audiences and families, stories with a fairly explicit moral or message are well received, such as "Roly-Poly Rice Ball," and "Drakes-Tail." Verbatim repetition is only acceptable to older children if it is done with humor or surprising changes.

All poems, and some stories—"Teeny-Tiny" and "The Cat and the Mouse," for example—need to be learned word-for-word. They have a chant-like quality that has a mesmerizing effect on young audiences. The learning of most stories, though, entails a combination of some exact memorization, along with a more general learning of basic sequence and structure. Thus, a storyteller can "know" a story very well, yet never tell it the same way twice. This is the way in which the artistry of the storyteller differs from that of the actor. The storyteller learns a story in a way that allows the telling to be adapted to suit a particular group and occasion, whereas the actor is tied to a fixed order of prerehearsed words and gestures.

We recommend that beginners choose tried-and-true stories, such as the ones in this book, then learn to tell them as close to the original as they can. Good stories have a structure that does not respond well to simplifying and paraphrasing. Making a story one's own—individualizing it—is a process of expanding, reworking, and enriching the story on the basis of experience telling it and living with it. Learn firsthand what elements of a story young children respond to before doing any improvising or personalization of it. In the process of telling many stories many times, you will develop a sense of story that will assist you in choosing new tales and adapting them to your own style and to the needs of different groups of children.

Most experienced storytellers use a combination of techniques for learning stories:

Word-for-word memorization. It's a good idea to memorize the first few sentences and the last few sentences of a story, as well as any rhymes, chants, magic words, character and place names, so that they roll effortlessly off your tongue.

Visualization. Create a mental map of most stories. Depending on the story, this can be a "bird's-eye view" from above, or a series of cinematic-style scenes. Actively visualizing the story's locale as you tell it gives an exciting immediacy to storytelling. Be careful, though, about adding too many descriptive details to a story for young children, who may not be able to visualize these details, and lose interest in the tale.

Structural outline. Learn to identify the scenes of the story and quickly run through them in your mind, in order. This is a sort of mental outlining, and you will become more adept at it as you progress.

Writing. We don't use this method, but several storytellers we know write the story they are learning in longhand.

Tape-recording. We find that the "language lesson" method works best for us, especially when we are pressed for time. Record a "meaningful unit" of the story (a sentence or two), leave enough blank space on the tape afterwards to allow yourself to repeat that portion of the story, then record the next sentence or two. Use the tape when driving, exercising, or doing housework, repeating each short sequence.

Private dress rehearsal. Sit or stand, visualize your audience before you, and tell the story from beginning to end—no starting over allowed.

STORYTELLING TECHNIQUE

Storytelling is more than knowing the words, of course. When you know the words, practice telling the story in front of the mirror. Use gestures that are familiar and comfortable. Shaking your head "yes" or "no," stirring a pot, putting something in your pocket, or showing how small something is with your fingers are simple and natural gestures that add to children's enjoyment and understanding of a story.

Tell stories in your natural, adult voice, slowing your pace, of course, for preschool children. Audiences generally appreciate character voices— in small doses! "The Three Bears" just wouldn't be "The Three Bears" if the storyteller didn't use different voices for each character. The bears' lines are quite short, so this is not a difficult task, even for a beginner. If you choose to use an unusual voice for the rooster in "The Elegant Rooster," or for the ant in "La Hormiguita," both of which entail long speeches, you could find yourself forced to tell most of the story in a voice that is difficult for you to sustain or project. Suggestions for the use of character voices are given with the storytelling instructions for each story. It isn't necessary to overdramatize

characters' emotions: a lowered, halting voice can usually express fear much better, for example, than trembling and shrieking.

THE STORYTELLING SPACE

Give thought in advance to the setting in which you will tell stories. An intimate arrangement, though not necessary, is always preferred, especially if teller or audience are new to storytelling. Try to use a space that is as quiet and private as possible. Arrange for the audience to sit in a semicircular configuration, even if they are seated in chairs. Most young children are comfortable on a carpeted floor. If at all possible, use a low to medium level of lighting. The teller must be physically close to the audience. Choose a seat that puts you just a bit higher than your listeners. If you are using puppets or a flannel board, sit in several different areas of the audience before the performance, and make sure that everyone will be able to see the props.

INTRODUCING A STORY

For a traditional storytelling audience, the words "once upon a time," or their local equivalent, signals that a story—exciting, magical, fictional—is about to begin. In contemporary school and library storytelling situations, more introduction is usually needed. Always tell your audience the origin— country, region, or tribe—of the story. This builds awareness of other cultures, and enhances the self-esteem of any children in the group who are from that culture. Words or concepts that will not be evident from their context in the story may need to be explained. The story of "Buchettino" features an ogre, for example, and we have found that many children have never heard of this fictional villain. Similarly, a stonecutter (in the story of the same name) is an occupation most children will not recognize, yet they may be able to guess what a stonecutter does, and imagine how large blocks of stone could be used. Involving children in such discussions before the storytelling stimulates active listening and encourages inferences of meaning from context.

DISCUSSING A STORY

Children should always be given the opportunity to comment on a story after it is told. They may respond emotionally saying that a particular character was mean or scary, for instance, or cognitively, suggesting other ways the characters could have behaved or telling how they themselves would have acted. One child's observation or question will often spark a group discussion, and the storyteller can participate subtly by "wondering" why or how something happened. The teller can also initiate a discussion with nondirective comments and questions.

When children have questions about a story, we find it best to ask if any of the other children have an answer before offering our own. No one is a final authority on the meaning of stories (though obvious misunderstandings may be corrected, of course). If we offer our own insights, we try to present them as being strictly our opinion, leaving the interpretation of the story as an open and ongoing process for the children.

PARTICIPATION

Participation in a story entails the audience either joining the storyteller in performing certain motions, saying words or phrases along with the storyteller, or supplying appropriate words or phrases at certain points in the story. This is a natural process and should be planned in such a way that the story can continue even if the children do not join in. It is seldom necessary to have the children rehearse their participation in advance. Young children will usually join in spontaneously or with only the slightest encouragement from the storyteller on repeated chants or refrains. Telling the story **twice** is usually preferable to a rehearsal and one telling. An exception would be a family story hour, in which adults would quickly learn the participatory element (such as the refrain in "Roly Poly Rice Ball") during a short rehearsal and help the children remember it during the retelling.

Children will be joining in on phrases or refrains that are repeated several times, thus the story itself provides ample opportunity to learn the words. Sometimes, participation will consist of guessing what happens next—usually from a predetermined set of three or four possibilities, such as in the story "Drakes-Tail." Or, the audience can join the storyteller in simple, expressive motions, such as the soldier stirring the soup pot in "Stone Soup."

Children can be invited to participate by an expectant pause on the part of the storyteller, an open-handed gesture, or by verbal encouragement, such as, "let's say it together." Participation must be enjoyable for the audience. It should also challenge their memory, or have an engaging cadence or rhyme. Young children can't resist repeating phrases or refrains spoken in an exaggerated character voice.

Telling Stories with the Flannel Board

Flannel board storytelling is a thriving contemporary art form. Teachers and librarians are constantly creating flannel board figures, telling tales, and exchanging ideas for this low-tech medium. For some odd reason, many writers on storytelling dismiss flannel boards as gimmicks that the "real" storyteller would never use. However, it is our experience that telling stories with the flannel board is a technique that enables more people to tell more stories to more children. In fact, it is often the *only* way to tell stories to young children, to students learning English, and to older and mixed-age groups unaccustomed to following a long narration. These are precisely the groups that many teachers and librarians are trying to reach.

Children five-years old and younger often have difficulty retaining the details of a story in memory long enough to get a feel for story structure and predict outcomes. The flannel board figures remind them of the story characters and setting, and, perhaps more important, keep their attention focused visually as they listen. Older children (and even adults) who are learning a new language can look to the flannel board for clues to story events and word meanings.

Only certain types of stories adapt well to the flannel board, such as cumulative tales ("The Elegant Rooster," "See for Yourself," and "The Hungry Cat") in which figures are added to a scene, one at a time, and all remain on the board until the end of the telling. Tales in which a series of characters play parallel, sequential roles in a scene, as in "The Goat in the Chile Patch," are also successful with the flannel board. "Teeny-Tiny" and "The Three Bears" have the appeal of dollhouse play to young children—they can see inside the houses as the characters sit on chairs, get dressed, or are tucked into bed. Short tales with few characters, such as "The Knee-High Man," "The Great Tug-o-War," and "Anansi and the Rock," make good flannel board stories. Acts of covering up and revealing, such as Brother Rabbit putting on a disguise, or the rock that crushes Anansi turning over to reveal dozens of little spiders, make good use of the flannel board's theatrical potential.

When using the flannel board, it is still necessary to learn—never read—the story. However, if you are sitting down to tell the story, with flannel board figures in your lap, you can discreetly hold a small card with brief notes on plot sequence, or to remind yourself of a refrain that needs to be repeated word-for-word. Always rehearse the placing and removing of figures, giving thought to the interplay between action and story. Timing is important, and can be used to surprise and delight the audience. Place a figure on the board before you name it and then pause. This gives the children a moment to guess its name, silently or aloud, offering them a chance to use predicting skills. When a character exits a scene abruptly—the goat in "The Goat in the Chile Patch," for example—sweep it off the board in a split second and place it out of sight.

MAKING A FLANNEL BOARD

Flannel boards may be purchased from educational and library supply companies. The fabric covering the flannel board should be black, a color that will contrast strongly with bright flannel board figures, allowing them to be seen from the greatest possible distance.

When making your own flannel board, choose a fabric that is fuzzy and synthetic. Synthetic fabrics produce the static electricity that makes figures adhere to the board. Acrylic fleece and robe velour, which can be found at most large fabric stores, are good choices. The fabric is then lapped and glued over a thin but strong rectangle of cardboard or pressboard. Such a simple, flat flannel board can be placed on a table-top or floor easel, or set in the tray of a chalkboard. Wherever you choose to place it, be sure that it tilts back at an angle, otherwise the figures will have a tendency to slide off.

We make our flannel boards from folding artist's portfolios, the kind with ribbon ties on three sides. With the two opposite sides tied together loosely, the board is self-supporting on a table top. (See Figure 1.) The fabric side of the board can be folded safely to the inside of the portfolio for carrying and storage, and folders containing the flannel board figures can also be carried inside. Portfolios are inexpensive, and are stocked by most art supply stores.

Figure 1. Table-top flannel board made from an artist's portfolio.

MAKING FLANNEL BOARD FIGURES

Copy the patterns for story figures from this book, enlarging or reducing them on a photocopy machine if you wish. There are several methods for making figures. The quickest is to trace the patterns directly onto white interfacing (nonwoven, nonfusible, medium to heavy weight). Interfacing is a basic sewing supply, and can be purchased at almost any fabric or variety store. It is transparent enough to trace through, and it readily accepts crayon, oil pastel, marker, and watercolor.

Be sure to color the figures before you cut them out, and to emphasize all lines on the figure with a medium-tip black permanent marker. Flannel board

figures made of interfacing are extremely durable and can be ironed flat if they become folded or wrinkled. **IMPORTANT:** When one figure will be placed on top of another on the flannel board, one of the two must be made of felt. Although figures made of interfacing will cling to the flannel board, they do not have enough loose fibers to adequately adhere to each other. For example, in order for the teeny-tiny woman to get into bed and pull up the covers, both bed and covers should be made of felt.

Some storytellers make all their figures from felt. The colors of felt are clear and bright, though the selection of colors is limited. Felt is especially useful when making large pieces of scenery that would be tedious to color on interfacing, such as trees or houses; felt pieces can be intermixed with ones made of interfacing in the same story set. The major disadvantage of felt is that its surface does not easily accept markers or paints. Thus, pieces of felt and trim must be glued to each figure to suggest clothing, hair, facial features, and so on. These add weight to each piece, making them more likely to slide off the flannel board. Felt also has a tendency to become limp and wrinkled with age, but it will stay crisp if you glue each figure to a backing piece of medium-weight interfacing. When gluing felt, always use a strong, flexible fabric glue, such as Sobo or Tacky.

Figures may also be made of lightweight paper and laminated between sheets of plastic. Color white paper with markers or crayons, or use fade-proof colored paper in a collage technique. On the back of each figure, place one or more rectangles, approximately one-half inch by one inch, of the hook component of adhesive-backed Velcro.

Keep the colors of your figures light and bright, for maximum contrast with the black background. Always make duplicates—even triplicates—of small pieces that could easily be misplaced, such as the grain of corn in "The Elegant Rooster."

Storytellers who like to draw cartoon figures can present some of our flannel board stories on the overhead projector. Those tales that accumulate one character after another work well—"The Elegant Rooster," "The Hungry Cat," and "See for Yourself." "La Hormiguita" can be drawn with the little ant represented as a dot, and her travels as a dotted line. This dotted line will also work for another ant story, "The Goat in the Chile Patch."

CHILDREN TELL STORIES WITH FLANNEL BOARDS

Children can make their own personal flannel boards by covering one half of the inside of a file folder with dark felt. The folder then serves both as flannel board and as storage for the figures. Children either use the figures on the storyteller's flannel board as models for their own drawings, or copy reductions of patterns in this book onto interfacing or felt. They can learn the story by telling it along with the storyteller, placing the figures on their individual boards as they follow along. Later, they can practice telling the story to each other, then take their flannel boards home to share their stories with their families.

Children can also use the full-sized figures and flannel board to tell stories, either informally, after the storytelling session, or as a more formal project. Working in teams of two, one child tells the story while the other places the figures on the board. Although this division of labor may not really be necessary, working in pairs helps overcome any shyness in performing in front of a group. Storytelling in pairs can also be used as a method of children teaching other children language through experiential learning. A proficient speaker of a language is paired as teller with another child who is not yet as proficient. The first child tells the story as the second child places the figures.

Telling Stories with Puppets

Blending puppetry with storytelling completely captures the attention of an audience of young children. They can easily pretend that the puppet on your hand is real, and will even blithely ignore the fact that you are speaking for the puppet. Use a subtle change of voice tone or pace for the puppet's voice. Interspersing a vocal "hook" in the dialogue can help you stay in character. When speaking as a tiger, for example, growl from time to time, or say "hmmmm" in a sneaky way for a tricky fox. Move the puppet as it speaks, and mime any of its motions. Practice your puppet actions in front of a mirror. When that particular character is not involved in the story, you can either put the puppet behind your back, a technique that is particularly appropriate if the character appears and disappears in the story, like the fox in "The Travels of a Fox," or you can simply hold the puppet still in a natural position, looking toward you, when it is not actively involved in the story.

Instructions are given with the stories "The Lion and the Mouse" and "Don't Let the Tiger Get You" for storytelling that involves two or more puppets.

CHILDREN'S PUPPET PLAYS

Children can use the flannel board patterns to make simple stick puppets. The story is then acted out informally in a circle, around a tabletop, or with a simple cardboard-box puppet stage. (See Resources for Storytelling for books on staging puppet plays.) Beginners can mime the story as you narrate. Pause to let them improvise the dialogue of the characters.

The patterns for felt hand puppets that accompany the stories "La Hormiguita," "The Travels of a Fox," and "Roly-Poly Rice Ball" may be adapted for the children's hand size. After an adult has sewn the two basic pieces together on a sewing machine, children can complete the puppets themselves, using felt scraps and white fabric glue.

PART 2
Folktales for Children
Two-and-a-half to Five

The Three Little Kittens (United States)

"The Three Little Kittens" is a traditional rhyme which first appeared in print in 1853 in a children's book published in the United States, *New Nursery Songs for All Good Children,* by Eliza Follen. It soon became a favorite Mother Goose rhyme, even though its pedigree can't be traced to earlier English collections.   It is not as nonsensical as other favorite nursery rhymes—the little kittens get into and out of trouble very much like real children.   Even though it is fairly long, its combination of rhyme and repetition help young children to learn it easily.

The three little kittens lost their mittens,
And they began to cry,
    "Oh, mother dear
    We sadly fear
    Our mittens we have lost."
    "What? Lost your mittens?
    You naughty kittens!
    You shall have no pie.
    Meow, meow, meow,
    You shall have no pie."
The three little kittens found their mittens
And they began to cry,
    "Oh, mother dear,
    Look here! Look here!
    Our mittens we have found."
    "What! Found your mittens?
    You good little kittens,
    Then you shall have some pie.
    Meow, meow, meow,
    You shall have some pie."

The three little kittens soiled their mittens,
And they began to cry,
    "Oh, mother dear
    We sadly fear
    Our mittens we have soiled."
    "What? Soiled your mittens?
    You naughty kittens!
    You shall have no pie.
    Meow, meow, meow,
    You shall have no pie."
The three little kittens washed their mittens,
And hung them out to dry.
    "Oh, mother dear,
    Look here! Look here!
    Our mittens we have washed."
    "What? Washed your mittens?
    You wonderful kittens!
    But hush, hush, hush,
    I smell a rat close by . . .
    Hush, hush, hush,
    I smell a rat close by."

FLANNEL BOARD STORYTELLING

"The Three Little Kittens" is a story-poem, and should be told in a way that highlights its rhythm and rhyme. Emphasize the word that is different in the first line of each stanza "lost . . . found . . . soiled . . . washed." This helps the children to understand the reason for the mother cat's reactions: angry, then pleased, then angry, then pleased.

Make three kitten flannel board figures by copying one of the kitten patterns once, the other twice. Mittens should be cut from brightly colored felt, and rubbed lightly on one side with a dark marker so that they can be turned over when they become soiled. Place them along an imaginary clothesline when the kittens hang them up to dry, then remove the mittens one pair at a time on the first "hush, hush, hush." Remove the kittens one at a time on the second "hush, hush, hush," and remove the mother on the final "I smell a rat close by." Ask the children what they think the mother cat will do about the rat.

PARTICIPATION

Children may already know some or all of this rhyme, and say it along with you. Tell it at least twice in a row, so that they have a chance to begin to learn the words. Encourage them to place a finger on their lips and join you on "hush, hush, hush."

LEADING TO READING

Look at and compare the illustrations of "The Three Little Kittens" in the picture book versions illustrated by Lorinda Bryan Cauley (Putnam, 1982), Paul Galdone (Clarion, 1986), Dorothy Stott (Putnam, 1984), and Shelley Thornton (Scholastic, 1986). Many Mother Goose anthologies also contain illustrations for this rhyme. *The Mitten*, a Russian folktale in picture book version adapted by Alvin Tresselt (Lothrop, 1964) and by Jan Brett (Putnam, 1989), is a story that takes place *inside* a mitten.

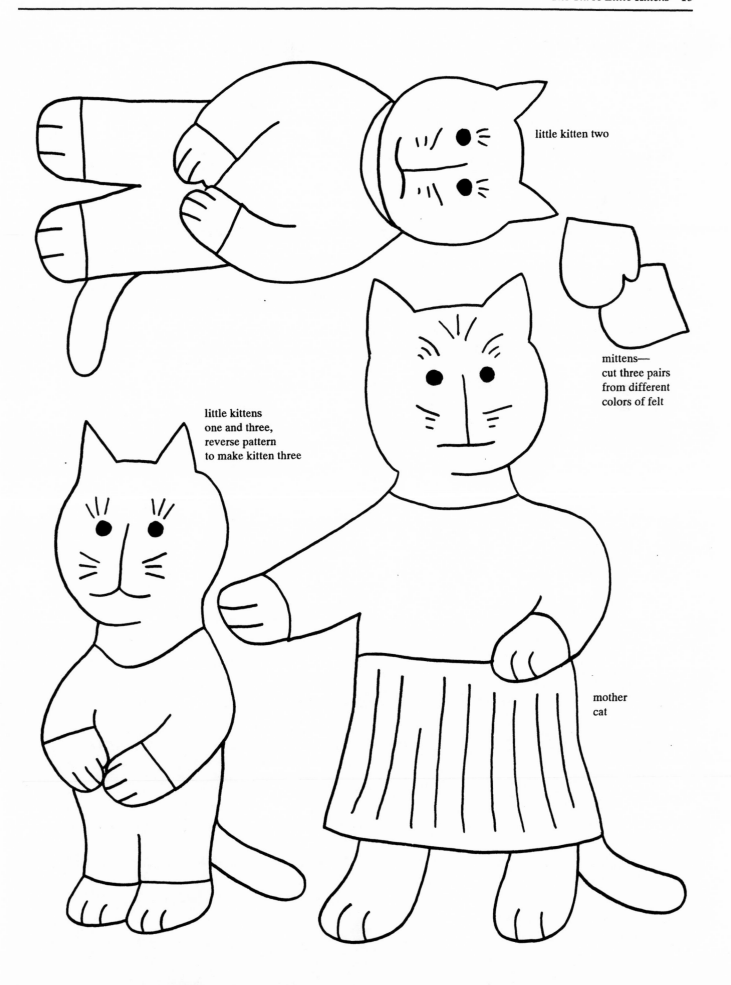

little kitten two

mittens—
cut three pairs
from different
colors of felt

little kittens
one and three,
reverse pattern
to make kitten three

mother
cat

Anna Mariah (Anglo-American)

There are many versions and variations on this rhyme—in some, "Jeremiah," or "Obadiah," or "Willie O'Dwyer" jump in the fire, and in one, "Little Jimmy Jack . . . sat on a tack!" In the oldest known English version,

> There was a man, and he went mad,
>
> He jumped into a paper bag . . .

The following is our own version, which we developed in an attempt to make the rhyme scheme last as long as possible, and to eliminate the obscure and obsolete words in many of the folk rhymes. Try making up your own series of rhyming jumps!

Anna Mariah
Jumped in the fire.
Fire was so hot,
She jumped in the pot.
Pot was so small,
She jumped on a ball.
Ball was so round,
She jumped on the ground.
Ground was so flat,
She jumped on the cat.
Cat was so scared,

She jumped on a chair.
Chair was so big,
She jumped on a pig.
Pig was so pink,
She jumped in the sink.
Sink was so narrow,
She jumped in a wheelbarrow.
Wheelbarrow was so red,
She jumped into bed.
Good night, Anna Mariah!

FLANNEL BOARD STORYTELLING

Using the flannel board makes learning and telling this story practically effortless. Place all the figures on the board before you begin to recite the poem, slowing down on the words "jumped in," then pausing briefly after "the," then picking up Anna Mariah and placing her above the fire just before you say the word "fire." The use of pause should be an integral part of the telling of this story, cuing the children to try to guess the rhyming word, which is also the name of the next place Anna Mariah jumps. Soon, some children will begin to make guesses as you pause, using the objects on the flannel board as clues. Don't worry, though, if some or all of them misidentify items, or don't seem to understand the rhyming scheme. This is a story to tell at least three or four times in a row. After the third telling most children will have mastered the text and will chant along confidently. Prior to the fourth telling, hand out the flannel board figures to members of your audience, leaving only Anna Mariah on the flannel board. This time, it is more difficult for the children to complete the rhymes since the visual cue—the flannel board figures—are not on the board. As the rhyme progresses, the child with the appropriate flannel board figure brings it up to you, and you place it on the board.

CHILDREN AS STORYTELLERS

Place the flannel board figures, except Anna Mariah, on the board, and have the children draw them on a sheet of paper. Then ask them to draw their own version of Anna Mariah on another piece of paper, cut it out, and tell the story themselves, making Anna jump around, from object to object, on their drawings.

LEADING TO READING

Three delightful picture books which, like "Anna Mariah," invite readers to guess the word that completes a rhyme are *Is Your Mama a Llama?* by Deborah Guarino (Scholastic, 1989), *It Does Not Say Meow*, by Beatrice Schenk de Regniers (Seabury, 1972), and *The Comical Adventures of Old Mother Hubbard and Her Dog*, illustrated by Tomie dePaola (Harcourt Brace, 1981).

Other folk versions of this rhyme can be found in Iona and Peter Opie's *Oxford Dictionary of Nursery Rhymes* (Oxford, 1951).

sink

ball

Anna Mariah

bed

pot

wheelbarrow

fire

cat

pig

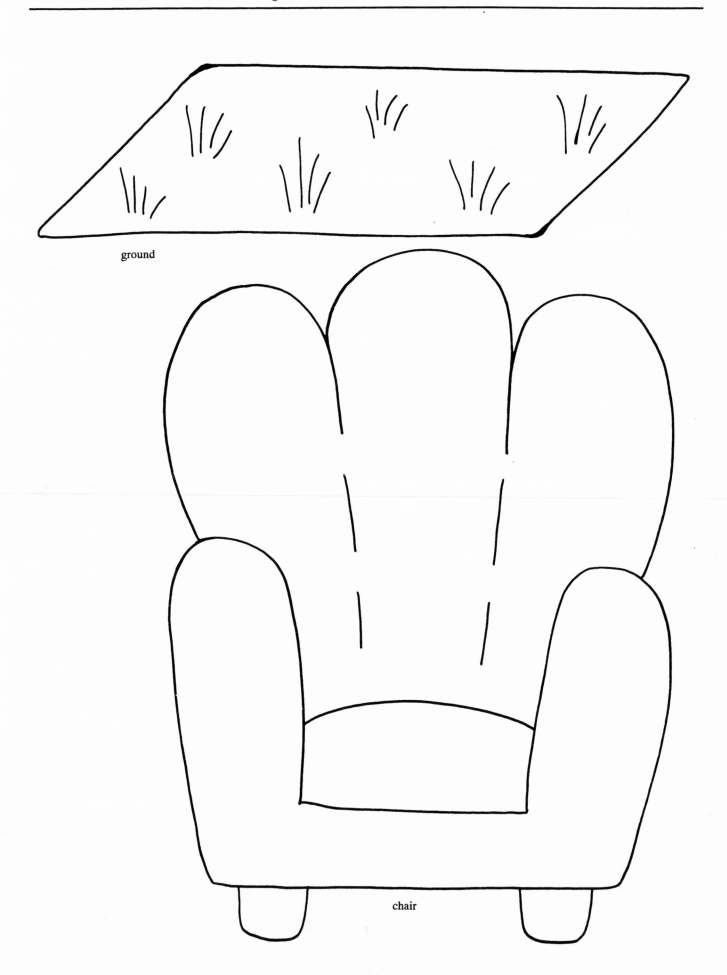

ground

chair

The Elegant Rooster (Spain)

"The Elegant Rooster" is a tale in which a chain reaction is carefully prepared by the storyteller, then set into motion in a rapid and highly satisfying conclusion. Young children delight in the cumulative repetition and rolling rhythm of the words. This folktale has been found in the oral tradition of Spain and Hispanic America; similar cumulative tales are known in other areas of Europe, and in Asia and Africa. A Spanish translation of this story can be found on page 24.

Early one morning, a rooster woke up and washed himself and preened himself until he was very, very clean and very, very elegant, and he set off for the wedding of Tío Perico. Along the way, he saw a grain of corn. What rooster can resist a grain of corn? But the grain of corn was right in the middle of a pile of garbage. The rooster wanted to eat the grain of corn. But he was on his way to the wedding of Tío Perico, and he didn't want to get dirty.

"I want to eat that grain of corn," he said, "but I won't, I won't, I won't."

"I want to eat that grain of corn . . . but I won't, I won't."

"I want to eat that grain of corn . . . but I won't."

At last, he couldn't help himself.

"**I want to eat that grain of corn!**," he said, and he picked up the grain of corn, and ate it. He got a tiny speck of dirt on his beak. Oh dear! He could never go to the wedding of Tío Perico with a dirty beak!

He looked around, and he saw a daisy by the side of the road.

"Daisy, please clean my beak, or I won't be able to go to the wedding of Tío Perico."

"*No quiero. No quiero*," said the daisy. "I don't want to."

The rooster looked around, and he saw a sheep.

"Sheep, eat this daisy. The daisy won't clean my beak, and I won't be able to go to the wedding of Tío Perico."

"*No quiero. No quiero*," said the sheep. "I don't want to."

The rooster looked around, and he saw a dog.

"Dog, bite this sheep. The sheep won't eat the daisy, the daisy won't clean my beak, and I won't be able to go to the wedding of Tío Perico."

"*No quiero. No quiero*," said the dog. "I don't want to."

The rooster looked around, and he saw a stick.

"Stick, beat this dog. The dog won't bite the sheep, the sheep won't eat the daisy, the daisy won't clean my beak, and I won't be able to go to the wedding of Tío Perico."

"*No quiero. No quiero*," said the stick. "I don't want to."

"The rooster looked around, and he saw a fire.

"Fire, burn this stick. The stick won't beat the dog, the dog won't bite the sheep, the sheep won't eat the daisy, the daisy won't clean my beak, and I won't be able to go to the wedding of Tío Perico."

"*No quiero. No quiero*," said the fire. "I don't want to."

The rooster looked around, and he saw some water.

"Water, put out this fire. The fire won't burn the stick, the stick won't beat the dog, the dog won't bite the sheep, the sheep won't eat the daisy, the daisy won't clean my beak, and I won't be able to go to the wedding of Tío Perico."

"No quiero. No quiero," said the water. "I don't want to."

The rooster looked around, and he saw the sun.

"Sun, dry up this water. The water won't put out the fire, the fire won't burn the stick, the stick won't beat the dog, the dog won't bite the sheep, the sheep won't eat the daisy, the daisy won't clean my beak, and I won't be able to go to the wedding of Tío Perico."

"I'll do what you ask," said the sun, "if you promise to crow three times every morning and wake me up."

"I promise," said the rooster.

And so. . .

The sun began to dry up the water.

The water began to put out the fire.

The fire began to burn the stick.

The stick began to beat the dog.

The dog began to bite the sheep.

The sheep began to eat the daisy.

The daisy cleaned the rooster's beak.

The rooster once again looked very, very clean and very, very elegant, and he went off to the wedding of Tío Perico. He ate and he danced and he had a wonderful time. He didn't get home until very late that evening. Still, he did not forget his promise to the sun.

And since then, every morning, the rooster crows,

> *Quiquiriqui*
>
> *Quiquiriqui*
>
> *Quiquiriqui*

And the sun wakes up!

FLANNEL BOARD STORYTELLING

Tell the children the title of the story and help them if they don't know what the word "elegant" means. Ask them if they understand what the Spanish words *no quiero* mean ("I don't want to"), and have them practice saying this phrase with you. Also rehearse making the noise of a Spanish speaking rooster: *quiquiriqui*

The flannel board figures will help you remember the sequence of this story. Be sure to arrange the figures in order before you begin; and always have a spare kernel of corn, or two, in case one gets lost. Place the rooster in the lower left-hand corner of the flannel board and the pile of garbage near the bottom center, so that the rooster can be moved closer to it after he notices the kernel of corn. When the rooster finally decides to eat the corn, remove it quickly from sight. The speck of dirt on his beak is imagi-

nary—emphasize to the children how small it is. (This explains why they can't see it.) Place the objects and characters that the rooster meets in a circular pattern, one by one counterclockwise on the board. (See Figure 2.) There is no need to move the rooster. When the final chain reaction of the tale begins, remove each figure as it is named.

PARTICIPATION

Encourage the children to guess the next character that the rooster will encounter by placing the figure on the flannel board before you name it. Also, invite them to join in saying the rooster's words by pausing before you say the name of each character, for example, "The water won't put out the (pause) fire, the fire won't burn the (pause) stick . . ." Signal them to join you in saying *"no quiero"* by shaking your head "no" each time the rooster asks a new character for help. Also pause before the rooster crows at the end of the story so that the audience may join you in crowing.

Figure 2. Flannel Board for the Elegant Rooster.

LEADING TO READING

Two picture books that retell similar "chain-reaction" folktales are the English tale, *Old Woman and Her Pig*, illustrated by Paul Galdone (Whittlesey, 1960), and the Irish *Munachar and Manachar!* illustrated by Anne Rockwell (Crowell, 1970). For help in locating other cumulative tales, see Margaret MacDonald's *Storyteller's Sourcebook* (Gale/Neal-Schuman, 1981).

El gallo elegante

Una mañana muy temprano, un gallo despertó, se bañó y se arregló hasta estar mucho muy limpio y mucho muy elegante y salió para ir a la boda del tío Perico. En el camino vio un granito de maíz.¿Qué gallo puede resistir el comerse un grano de maíz? Pero el granito de maíz estaba en medio de un montón de basura. El gallo quería comerse el granito. Pero iba rumbo a la boda del tío Perico y no quería ensuciarse.

—Quiero comerme el granito de maíz — decía — pero no, no, no me lo como. — Quiero comerme el granito de maíz . . . pero no, no me lo como.—

— Quiero comerme el granito de maíz . . . pero no me lo como.—

Por fin, no pudo resistir la tentación.

—**Quiero commerme ese grano de maiz!**— dijo, y tomó el granito de maíz y se lo comió. En su pico había una manchita. —¡Dios mio!— No podía ir a la boda con el pico sucio!

Miró a su alrededor, y vio una margarita al lado del camino.

—Margarita, por favor limpia mi pico, si no, no podré ir a la boda del tío Perico

— No quiero, no quiero — dijo la margarita. —No quiero limpiarte el pico.

El gallo miró a su alrededor y vio a un borrego.

—Borrego, cómete la margarita. Ella no quiere limpiarme el pico, y yo no podré ir a la boda del tío Perico.

— No quiero. No quiero — dijo el borreguito. —No quiero comerme la margarita.

El gallo miró a su alrededor y vio a un perro.

— Perro, muerde al borrego. El borrego no quiere comerse la margarita, la margarita no quiere limpiarme el pico, y yo no podré ir a la boda del tío Perico.

— No quiero. No quiero — dijo el perro — No quiero morder al borrego.

El gallo miró a su alrededor y vio un palo.

— Palo, pégale al perro. El perro no quiere morder al borrego, el borrego no quiere comerse la margarita, la margarita no quiere limpiarme el pico, y yo no podré ir a la boda del tío Perico. —

—No quiero. No quiero — dijo el palo.— No quiero pegarle al perro —

El gallo miró a su alrededor y vio una lumbre.

— Lumbre, quema el palo. El palo no quiere pegarle al perro, el perro no quiere morder al borrego, el borrego no quiere comerse la margarita, la margarita no quiere limpiarme el pico, y yo no podré ir a la boda del tío Perico—

—No quiero. No quiero — dijo la lumbre — No quiero quemar el palo —

El gallo miró a su alrededor y vio el agua.

— Agua, apaga la lumbre. La lumbre no quiere quemar el palo, el palo no quiere pegarle al perro, el perro no quiere morder al borrego, el borrego no quiere comerse la margarita, la margarita no quiere limpiarme el pico, y yo no podré ir a la boda del tío Perico —

— No quiero. No quiero — dijo el agua — No quiero apagar la lumbre —

El gallo miró hacia arriba y vio el sol.

—Sol, seca el agua. El agua no quiere apagar la lumbre, la lumbre no quiere quemar el palo, el palo no quiere pegarle al perro, el perro no quiere morder al borrego, el borrego no quiere comerse la margarita, la margarita no quiere limpiarme el pico, y yo no podré ir a la boda del tío Perico.

— Haré lo que me pides — dijo el sol — si me prometes cantar tres veces cada mañana para despertarme —

—Te lo prometo — dijo el gallo.

En eso. . .

El sol empezó a secar el agua.

El agua empezó a apagar la lumbre.

La lumbre empezó a quemar el palo.

El palo empezó a pegarle al perro.

El perro empezó a morder al borrego.

El borrego empezó a comerse la margarita.

La margarita le limpió el pico al gallo.

Una vez más el gallo se veía mucho muy limpio, y mucho muy elegante, y se fue rumbo a la boda del tío Perico. Comió y bailó y se divirtió muchísimo. No llegó a su casa sino hasta muy noche. Sin embargo, no olvidó su promesa al sol.

Y desde entonces, cada mañana, el gallo canta,

¡Quiquiriquí!

¡Quiquiriquí!

¡Quiquiriquí!

¡Y el sol despierta!

Translated by Adela Artola Allen

kernel
of
corn

water

rooster

dog

sun

garbage

fire

daisy

stick

sheep

The Three Bears (England)

"The Three Bears" does not appear in folk tradition outside the British Isles, and in early published variants, the intruder was not a little girl, but an old woman, or a fox. Goldilocks first appeared as a tale character in the book *Old Nursery Stories and Rhymes*, illustrated by John Hassall, published circa 1904. The story's highly repetitive plot, and its small, medium, and large characters, make it easy for storytellers to tell, and for listeners to remember.

Once upon a time there were three bears who lived together in a house in the woods. One of them was a wee small bear, one was a middle-sized bear, and the other was a great big bear. They each had a bowl for their porridge—a little bowl for the wee small bear, a middle-sized bowl for the middle-sized bear, and a great big bowl for the great big bear. And they each had a chair to sit in—a little chair for the wee small bear, and a middle-sized chair for the middle-sized bear, and a great big chair for the great big bear. And they each had a bed to sleep in—a wee small bed for the wee small bear, and a middle-sized bed for the middle-sized bear, and a great big bed for the great big bear.

One day, after they had made the porridge for their breakfast, and scooped it out into their bowls, they walked out into the wood while the porridge was cooling, so that they wouldn't burn their mouths by starting to eat it too soon. And while they were out walking, a little girl named Goldilocks came to the house. She looked in at the window, and she peeked in at the door, and seeing nobody in the house, she lifted the latch and went inside.

First, she tasted the porridge of the great big bear, and it burned her mouth. It was too hot! Then, she tasted the porridge of the middle-sized bear. Oh, it was too cold. Then she went to the porridge of the wee small bear, and tasted that, and it was neither too hot, nor too cold, but just right, and she liked it so well that she ate it all up.

Then Goldilocks sat down in the chair of the great big bear, but it was too hard. Then she sat in the chair of the middle-sized bear, but it was too soft for her. Then she sat down in the chair of the wee small bear, and it was just right. She sat and she rocked and she rocked and she rocked so much that the bottom fell out and she fell on the ground.

Then Goldilocks went upstairs to the bedroom of the three bears. And first she lay down upon the bed of the great big bear, but it was too hard. Then she lay down upon the bed of the middle-sized bear, but that bed was too soft. So she lay down upon the bed of the wee small bear, and that was just right. So she put her head on the pillow and fell fast asleep.

By this time, those three bears thought their porridge would be cool enough for them to eat, so they came home to breakfast. Now, Goldilocks had left the spoon of the great big bear standing in the bowl of porridge.

"Someone has been eating my porridge," said the great big bear in his great big voice.

The middle-sized bear looked at her porridge, and the spoon was standing in her bowl, too.

"Someone has been eating my porridge," said the middle-sized bear in her middle-sized voice.

Then the wee small bear looked at his bowl, and there was his spoon, but the porridge was all gone.

"Someone has been eating my porridge, and has eaten it all up!" said the wee small bear in his wee small voice.

Then the three bears began to look about, and the great big bear saw that someone had pushed aside the cushion in his great big chair.

"Someone has been sitting in my chair," said the great big bear in his great big voice.

The middle-sized bear saw that someone had squashed down the cushion in her chair.

"Someone has been sitting in my chair," said the middle-sized bear in her middle-sized voice.

And you know what Goldilocks had done to the chair of the wee small bear.

"Someone has been sitting in my chair, and has sat it all to pieces," said the wee small bear in his wee small voice.

Then the three bears went upstairs to their bedroom. Goldilocks had wrinkled up the covers on the great big bed.

"Someone has been sleeping in my bed," said the great big bear in his great big voice. And the middle-sized bear saw that the pillow was pushed aside on her bed.

"Someone has been sleeping in my bed," said the middle-sized bear in her middle-sized voice.

And then, the wee small bear went to look at his bed.

"Someone has been sleeping in my bed, and **there she is!**" said the wee small bear in his wee small voice.

Goldilocks opened her eyes and saw the furry faces of the three bears looking down at her. She jumped out of bed, and she climbed out the window, and she never again went to the house of the three bears.

FLANNEL BOARD STORYTELLING

Make the table of gray or brown felt. Choosing a different bright color for each bear, color code their bowls, chairs, and beds. This will give children two cues (size and color) as to the rightful owner of each item Goldilocks disturbs. Glue the bowls to the table. Cut the wee small bear's chair on the dotted line. Carefully place the chair on the flannel board so the cut is not obvious to the audience; then, when Goldilocks sits on the chair pull it apart so that it clearly looks broken. Set up the table, chairs, and beds on the flannel board so as to resemble the interior of a two story house, as illustrated in Figure 3. The three bears lie on their three beds as you begin telling the story.

Figure 3. Flannel Board for theThree Bears.

PARTICIPATION

Many children know at least some of this story. Encourage them, through eye contact and nodding your head in approval, to join you in identifying each bowl, chair, and bed at the beginning of the tale, and in speaking along with the bears as they discover what is amiss in their house.

LEADING TO READING

Several picture books retell the story of "The Three Bears," including Paul Galdone's straightforward version (Seabury, 1972), and, for those who already know the story, James Marshall's updated comic *Goldilocks and the Three Bears* (Dial, 1988). Poems about Goldilocks and the three bears can be found in Jane Yolen's *Three Bears Rhyme Book* (Harcourt, Brace, 1987).

wee-small bear

Goldilocks

middle-sized
bear

great big
bear

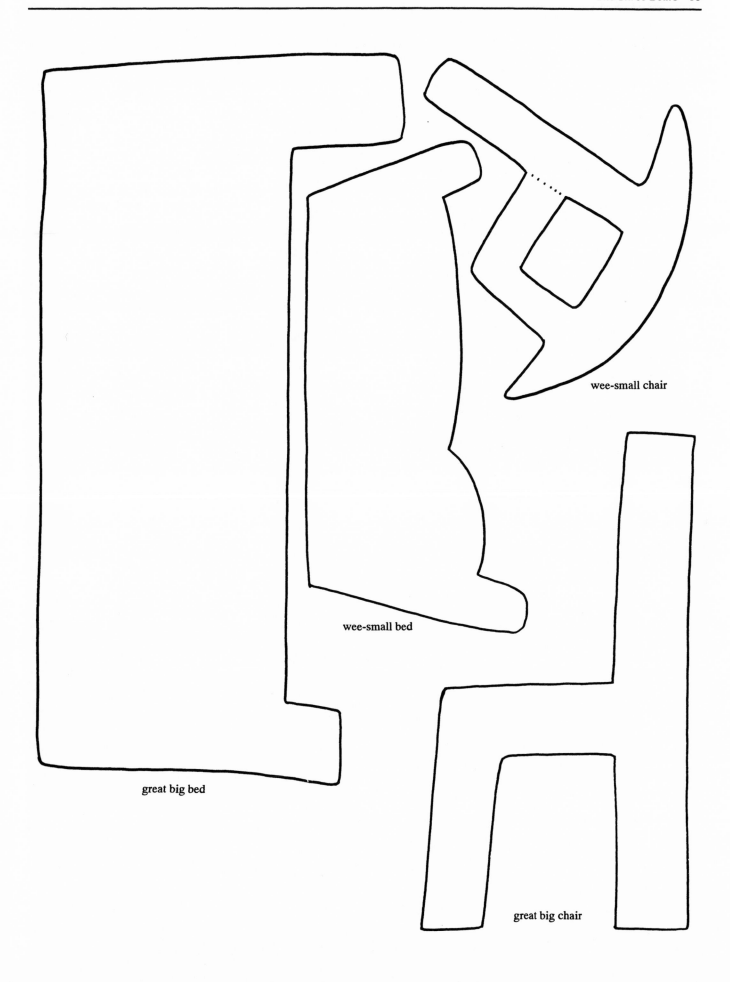

wee-small chair

wee-small bed

great big bed

great big chair

middle-sized chair

middle-sized bed

table

great big bowl

middle-sized bowl

wee-small bowl

The Cat and the Mouse (England)

This cumulative folktale from English tradition begins with a sad event—a mouse losing her tail—and ends happily, thanks to the little mouse's skill and perseverance at making a series of trades. The sequence of causes and effects challenges children's minds, and the cumulative repetition helps them keep track of what has happened so far in the story.

The cat and the mouse
Play'd in the malt-house:

The cat bit the mouse's tail off. "Pray, puss, give me my tail." "No," says the cat, "I'll not give you your tail, till you go to the cow, and fetch me some milk."

First she leapt and then she ran
Till she came to the cow, and thus began:

"Pray, cow, give me milk, so that I may give cat milk, so that cat may give me my own tail again." "No," said the cow, "I will give you no milk, till you go to the farmer, and get me some hay."

First she leapt, and then she ran
Till she came to the farmer, and thus began:

"Pray, farmer, give me hay, so that I may give cow hay, so that cow may give me milk, so that I may give cat milk, so that cat may give me my own tail again." "No," says the farmer, "I'll give you no hay, till you go to the butcher and fetch me some meat."

First she leapt, and then she ran,
Till she came to the butcher, and thus began:

"Pray, butcher, give me meat, so that I may give farmer meat, so that farmer may give me hay, so that I may give cow hay, so that cow may give me milk, so that I may give cat milk, so that cat may give me my own tail again."

"No," says the butcher, "I'll give you no meat, till you go to the baker and fetch me some bread."

First she leapt, and then she ran,
Till she came to the baker, and thus began:

"Pray, baker, give me bread, so that I may give butcher bread, so that butcher may give me meat, so that I may give farmer meat, so that farmer may give me hay, so that I may give cow hay, so that cow may give me milk, so that I may give cat milk, so that cat may give me my own tail again."

Yes, says the baker, I'll give you some bread,

But if you eat my grain, I'll cut off your head!

Then. . .

the baker gave mouse bread,

and mouse gave butcher bread,

butcher gave mouse meat,

and mouse gave farmer meat,

and farmer gave mouse hay,

and mouse gave cow hay,

and cow gave mouse milk,

and mouse gave cat milk,

and cat gave mouse her own tail again.

FLANNEL BOARD STORYTELLING

Place the mouse on the lower left of the flannel board, making her removable tail look like it is attached to her body. Position the cat just to the right of the mouse. When mouse's tail is bitten off place it in the cat's upraised paw. Put the cow in the upper left corner, the farmer upper center, the butcher upper right, and the baker bottom right, each as they are named in the story. (See Figure 4.) Then, make the mouse leap to a spot just in front of each. When the mouse begins her return rounds—giving something to each character—merely tap that character with the mouse figure. There are no actual flannel board pieces for milk, bread, meat, etc., and our audiences have been quite content imagining them.

Figure 4. Flannel Board for the Cat and the Mouse.

PARTICIPATION

Encourage participation by pausing for the children to remember exactly what it was that the mouse needed to get from each character:

The baker gave the mouse (pause) *bread,*

The mouse gave the butcher bread,

The butcher gave the mouse (pause). . .

Don't pause too long, or you'll lose the rhythm of the story, but do allow for an extended pause after, "and cat gave mouse her own . . . tail," so that the children can finish the story with you.

LEADING TO READING

Children are fascinated with the idea of making trades. *The Piney Woods Peddler*, by George Shannon (Greenwillow, 1981), and *The Swapping Boy*, by John Langstaff (Harcourt Brace, 1960) are two tales that tell of a long series of exchanges. Both have irresistible refrains to sing or chant along. To locate folktales similar to "The Cat and the Mouse" from other cultures, see Margaret MacDonald's *Storyteller's Sourcebook* (Gale/Neal-Schuman, 1981).

mouse's tail

mouse

cow

farmer

cat

butcher

baker

The Goat in the Chile Patch
(United States: Hispanic)

The billy goat's stubbornness in this New Mexican folktale is similar to that of the characters encountered in "The Elegant Rooster." Both tales pose the question, "How do you go about getting someone to do what you want?" The tale of the goat who wouldn't leave the garden is known throughout Europe and the Americas; the goat's taste for chile peppers gives this particular variant a Southwestern flavor. Young children enjoy the clear sense of justice in the story. They laugh when the storyteller tells them the goat won't go near the garden again. A Spanish translation follows on page 42.

Once, a man and a woman lived on a farm. In their garden, they grew all sorts of vegetables, but their favorite vegetables of all were green chile peppers. Now, one day the big billy goat broke through the fence and got into their garden and started eating all the ripe chiles.

The man and the woman ran outside as fast as they could and they tried to chase the billy goat out of the garden. They shouted and they pushed and they pulled, but they just couldn't make him leave. So they asked the rooster to help them.

The rooster flew at the goat, squawking and pecking.

"Get out of the chile patch!" the rooster screeched.

"No, **you** get out," said the billy goat, and he kicked the rooster up in the air.

And the billy goat went right on eating the chiles.

So the man and the woman asked the dog to help them.

The dog ran toward the goat, barking and growling.

"Get out of the chile patch!" yelped the dog.

"No, **you** get out," said the billy goat, and he kicked the dog up in the air.

And the billy goat went right on eating the chiles.

So the man and the woman asked the bull to help them.

The bull snorted and pawed at the ground and gave the goat his meanest look.

"Get out of the chile patch!" bellowed the bull.

"No, **you** get out," said the billy goat, and he kicked the bull up in the air.

And the billy goat went right on eating the chiles.

Along came a little red ant.

"I think I can make that billy goat get out of your chile patch," said the ant.

"How can a little ant do something that the rooster, and the dog, and even the bull couldn't do?" said the man and the woman.

"Just watch me," said the ant.

The ant walked over to the billy goat.

The goat didn't even see the ant coming.

The ant walked up the billy goat's back leg.

The goat didn't even feel the ant walking.

The ant walked along the billy goat's back.

The goat still didn't feel the ant.

The ant walked across the soft skin behind the billy goat's ear, and . . . **bit** the billy goat.

The billy goat jumped up into the air, and ran out of the garden as fast as he could. And do you know? He never, ever went near that chile patch again.

FLANNEL BOARD STORYTELLING

Place the chiles in the center of the flannel board. Put the man to the left, the woman to the right of the chile patch as each is mentioned, then set the goat in the middle of the plants. When the man and woman attempt to chase the goat away, move them closer to him. Then, when they fail to make him leave, place them in the lower corners of the flannel board. The rooster, dog, and bull are placed beside the goat until the moment when he sends each of them flying. Animate their departure with a somersault and a loud squawk/yelp/bellow, then place them along the bottom edge of the board, between the man and woman.

There is no flannel board figure for the ant—it's too small to see. As you describe its travels, trace its path with your finger. Pause to allow children to guess what the ant will do after it reaches the soft skin behind the billy goat's ear (bite!). Then, quickly remove the figure of the goat from the flannel board, keeping him out of sight while you finish telling the story. On a second telling, invite the children to join in on the billy goat's lines, "No, **you** get out!"

LEADING TO READING

Two picture-book tales in which the smallest creature has the biggest impact are *The Napping House* by Audrey Wood (Harcourt Brace, 1984), and in the Russian folktale, *The Great Big Enormous Turnip*, retold by Helen Oxenbury (Watts, 1968).

El cabrito en la hortaliza de los chiles

Había una vez un hombre y una mujer que vivían en un rancho. En la hortaliza, tenían muchas verduras; entre ellas, sus predilectas eran los chiles verdes. Un día, el cabrito tumbó el cerco, entró a la hortaliza y empezó a comerse todos los chiles.

El hombre y la mujer salieron corriendo al ver lo que pasaba y trataron de sacar al cabrito de la hortaliza. Le pegaron de gritos, lo empujaron para allá y para acá pero no lograron sacarlo. Así que le pidieron ayuda al gallo.

El gallo se dirigió al cabrito picándolo y cacareando—¡salte de la hortaliza y deja los chiles!—gritaba el gallo.

—No, salte tú - dijo el cabrito—y le dió una patada al gallo que lo lanzó por el aire.

Y el cabrito siguió comiéndose los chiles.

El hombre y la mujer le pidieron ayuda al perro.

El perro se enfrentó con el cabrito gruñendo y ladrando.

—¡Salte de la hortaliza y deja los chiles! - ladraba el perro.

—No, salte tú - dijo el cabrito—y le dió una patada que lo lanzó por el aire.

El hombre y la mujer le pidieron ayuda al buey.

El buey bufando y pateando le echó su más amenazante mirada al cabrito.

—¡Salte de la hortaliza y deja los chiles!—bufó el buey.

—No, salte tú - dijo el cabrito - y le dió una patada al buey que lo lanzó por el aire.

Y el cabrito siguió comiéndose los chiles.

En eso llegó una hormiguita.

—Creo que puedo hacer al cabrito salir de la hortaliza - dijo la hormiguita.

—¿Cómo puede una hormiguita lograr lo que el gallo, y el perro y hasta el buey no pudieron?—dijeron el hombre y la mujer.

—Véanme - dijo la hormiguita

La hormiguita se dirigió al cabrito.

El cabrito ni siquiera vió que venía.

La hormiguita se trepó por la pata trasera del cabrito.

El cabrito no sintió nada.

La hormiguita atravesó la espalda del cabrito.

El cabrito todavía no sentía nada.

La hormiguita llegó hasta la suave piel detrás de la oreja del cabrito y ahí lo mordió.

El cabrito dió un salto en el aire, y salió corriendo de la hortaliza Y, ¿sabes qué? Nunca, jamás, volvió a la hortaliza.

Translated by Adela Artola Allen

chiles

billy goat

rooster

man

woman

dog

bull

Anansi and the Rock (West Africa)

Tales about Anansi the spider from West African and African-American sources are especially popular in children's folklore collections and picture books. In "Anansi and the Rock," a tale from Ghana, the trickster-hero has difficulty controlling his greed, and is fittingly punished. The "how and why" ending of "Anansi and the Rock" is typical of many African folktales, and does not indicate that storytellers or their audiences believed it to be a true explanation of natural events, e.g., that spiders live under rocks. Rather, it playfully signals the end of the story.

Once there was a famine in the land where Anansi the spider lived. Everyone in Anansi's village was weak from hunger. Anansi lived in misery. When people said they wished they had some yams to eat, Anansi m-o-a-n-e-d. When they said they would sure appreciate some good spicy beans, Anansi g-r-o-a-n-e-d. When people said how delicious even a tiny millet cake would taste, Anansi moaned, and groaned, and held his stomach in agony.

Anansi went hunting one day with the pig and the antelope. They hunted all morning, but they didn't see any game. They hunted all afternoon, but they didn't see any game. They hunted until the sun went down. Still nothing. They sat down in a clearing beside a smooth flat rock.

"That rock looks special," said the pig.

"It looks like a grinding stone," said Anansi.

"It might be a stone for grinding millet," said antelope.

Instantly, the stone began to turn around and around, and then a large sack of millet flour appeared on top of it.

The antelope took the sack.

"I would like some millet flour, also," said the pig.

The stone turned around and around, and ground out a sackful of millet flour for the pig.

The pig and the antelope looked at Anansi. They were waiting for him to ask for his flour. But Anansi said, "I am going to take this stone back to my house, and keep it for myself."

Anansi lifted the stone.

"Spider! Spider! Put me down!" said the stone.

Anansi put the stone on his head.

"Spider! Spider! Put me down," said the stone.

Anansi began to walk with the stone on his head.

> "Antelope took enough and let me be.
> Pig took enough and let me be.
> Spider! Spider! Put me down!"

But Anansi just kept on walking. Slowly the stone began to turn around and around, around and around. Anansi tried to push the stone off his head, but it was stuck there. It turned around and around, around and around, around and around, until it ground Anansi down into the grass, and crushed him into a thousand tiny pieces. Each piece turned into a tiny spider. That is why today, when you lift up a big rock, you will see so many little spiders living there.

FLANNEL BOARD STORYTELLING

The rock in the story should be made of light-gray or light-brown felt. Cut out many baby spiders (asterisk shapes) from dark felt and glue them to one side of the rock with fabric glue.

Begin the telling with Anansi on the left side of the flannel board. At the appropriate point in the story, place the antelope to Anansi's right, and the pig to the antelope's right, allowing space between the pig and the antelope for the rock. As the antelope and the pig wait for Anansi to ask the rock for some millet, switch the figures of the antelope and Anansi. As Anansi is being crushed down by the rock, use your fingertips to slowly work the flannel board figure of Anansi into your palm while moving the rock downward with the other hand. On the words, "That is why today, when you lift up a big rock ...," turn the rock over and place it quickly on the flannel board to reveal the tiny spiders.

PARTICIPATION

Make a large circular arm motion, parallel to the ground, on the words "around and around," and motion for the children to join you saying the words and performing the action. On a second telling, without the flannel board, ask the children to pretend they are Anansi, being crushed down, down, down, by the rock. When you clap your hands, they will change into many, tiny spiders (most will make their hands and even feet into spiders). Clap again, and tell them to change back into themselves.

LEADING TO READING

Three picture books—all great read-alouds with exciting illustrations—tell of other adventures of Anansi: *Anansi the Spider*, by Gerald McDermott (Holt, 1972), *Anansi and the Moss-Covered Rock*, by Eric A. Kimmel (Holiday, 1988), and *A Story, A Story*, by Gail E. Haley (Atheneum, 1970).

bag of
millet flour

pig

antelope

Anansi

rock

La Hormiguita (Mexico)

The folktale of the little ant is widely known in Spain and Latin America. In most versions, this tiny heroine's search for justice ends with her being sent to someone so powerful and terrifying that she decides to abandon her quest. In some folk variants, this power is God, in others, Death. For young children, we find that the anteater fills this role nicely. A Spanish translation of this story begins on page 52.

━━━━━━━━━━━━━━

Early one morning in spring of the year, *la hormiguita*, the little ant baked a loaf of bread to take to her godmother. She left her house, carrying the bread, and set off down the road,

    pum   pum   pum   pum

        pum   pum   pum   pum

She stepped on a tiny drop of water. She didn't know it, but that drop of water was frozen solid.

WHEEEEE!

The little ant slipped on the ice.

BAM!

She landed on the ground, and she hurt her foot, and the bread fell into the dirt. Now the little ant had no bread to take to her godmother. She sat in the road and rubbed her foot.

Along came *el grillo,* the cricket.

"What happened?" the cricket asked.

"I slipped on the ice, and hurt my foot, and dropped the loaf of bread I baked for my godmother," said the ant.

"That," said the cricket, "is the fault of *la escarcha,* the frost. Frost froze the drop of water, the drop of water turned into ice, the ice made you slip. Go and ask the frost for justice."

So the little ant, *la hormiguita*, set off to find the frost,

    pum   pum   pum   pum

        pum   pum   pum   pum

And when she found the frost, she said, "I demand justice. You froze ice, ice made me slip and hurt my foot, and drop the loaf of bread I baked for my godmother."

"No, no, it wasn't my fault," said the frost. "There is one much stronger than I am—*el sol*, the sun, makes me melt. Go and ask the sun for justice."

So the little ant set off to find the sun,

    pum   pum   pum   pum

        pum   pum   pum   pum

And when she found the sun, she said, "I demand justice. You melt frost, frost freezes ice, ice made me slip and hurt my foot, and drop the loaf of bread I baked for my godmother."

"No, no, it wasn't my fault," said the sun. "There is one much stronger than I am. *La nube*, the cloud, covers up my face. Go and ask the cloud for justice."

So the little ant set off to find the cloud,

pum   pum   pum   pum

pum   pum   pum   pum

And when she found the cloud, she said, "I demand justice. You cover sun, sun melts frost, frost freezes ice, ice made me slip and hurt my foot, and drop the loaf of bread I baked for my godmother."

"No, no, it wasn't my fault," said the cloud. "There is one much stronger than I am. *El viento*, the wind, pushes me right out of the sky. Go and ask the wind for justice."

So the little ant set off to find the wind,

pum   pum   pum   pum

pum   pum   pum   pum

And when she found the wind, she said, "I demand justice. You push cloud, cloud covers sun, sun melts frost, frost freezes ice, ice made me slip and hurt my foot, and drop the loaf of bread I baked for my godmother."

"No, no, it wasn't my fault," said the wind. "There is one much stronger than I. *La pared*, the wall, stops me dead in my tracks. Go and ask the wall for justice."

So the little ant set off to find the wall,

pum   pum   pum   pum

pum   pum   pum   pum

And when she found the wall, she said, "I demand justice. You stop wind, wind pushes cloud, cloud covers sun, sun melts frost, frost freezes ice, ice made me slip and hurt my foot, and drop the loaf of bread I baked for my godmother."

"No, no, it wasn't my fault," said the wall. "There is one much stronger than I. *El comején* the termite is eating me up. Go and ask the termite for justice."

So the little ant set off to find the termite,

pum   pum   pum   pum

pum   pum   pum   pum

And when she found the termite, she said, "I demand justice. You eat wall, wall stops wind, wind pushes cloud, cloud covers sun, sun melts frost, frost freezes ice, ice made me slip and hurt my foot, and drop the loaf of bread I baked for my godmother.

"No, no, it wasn't my fault," said the termite. "There is one much stronger than I. *El oso hormiguero* sends out his long, sticky tongue to catch me. Go and ask him for justice."

So the little ant set out to find *el oso hormiguero*,

pum   pum   **oh no!**

pum   pum

The little ant remembered what her mother had told her about *el oso hormiguero*. . .

He is the **anteater.**

"I'd better not ask *el oso hormiguero* for justice," said the little ant to herself. Instead, she tied a bandage around her foot, and dusted off the loaf of bread, and set off to her godmother's house,

pum   pum   pum   pum

pum   pum   pum   pum

She never did get justice. But at least she didn't get

Eaten!

FLANNEL BOARD STORYTELLING

Begin the telling by placing the ant at the top center of the flannel board, and add the characters she encounters in a counterclockwise pattern, always leaving a space for her to stand to the *right* of each. Each time she travels to meet a new character, move her so that she faces it. Use crayon or marker to make one side of the loaf of bread look dirty. You will flip it over when she drops it, and again, at the end of the story, when she brushes it off. Place each new character on the board after saying its name in Spanish and before saying it in English. This serves two purposes: first, it gives Spanish-speaking children a bit of a head start in predicting the course of the action, and second, it builds a language lesson into the tale telling.

We don't use a flannel board figure for the anteater. Instead we use an anteater puppet (see instructions below). We remove *la hormiguita* from the board, and ask the children if they would like to see *el oso hormiguero.* He appears over the top of the flannel board and waves to the children. He can then conduct a friendly Spanish quiz, pointing to each figure on the flannel board with his nose, and waiting for the children to say its name in Spanish.

Figure 5. Flannel board for La Hormiguita.

Anteater Puppet

Draw a pattern like the one in Figure 6, using your hand as a model. The two smaller fingers bend forward and down when inside the puppet. They are shown stretched out to the side in the drawing, since this is what the flat pattern will look like. Roll your hand from one side to the other while tracing it onto

paper. Add one-half inch all around for the seam. Cut two pieces of felt or other fairly thick fabric, soft or fuzzy. Stitch the two halves together, leaving the bottom open and turn. Glue on felt eyes and a long, pink felt tongue. To make the anteater's ears stand up, cut them from good, thick felt, or from a colored sponge. Put the puppet on your hand, and bend your first two fingers down into the nose. The ears should be placed right on top of the fold made by your knuckles. Glue the ears in place with contact cement (for sponge) or strong fabric glue such as Tacky or Sobo (for felt). Some actions the anteater puppet can perform well are waving, clapping, and nodding its head up and down rapidly for an enthusiastic "yes!" To mime "no," a hand puppet must turn its whole body (rotate your wrist left and right).

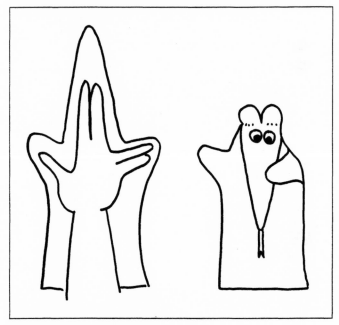

Figure 6. Anteater hand puppet.

LEADING TO READING

Passing the blame along a chain of animals is the theme of Verna Aardema's retelling of the African Folktale, *Why Mosquitos Buzz in People's Ears* (Dial, 1975), and of Helen Lester's picture book, *It Wasn't My Fault* (Houghton Mifflin, 1985). Compare the sequence of characters and their actions in these two to those in "La Hormiguita." You may also want to stage a simple puppet play of the Filipino folktale on the same theme, "Why Mosquitos Buzz in Our Ears," in *Fantastic Theater: Puppets and Plays for Young Players and Young Audiences*, by Judy Sierra (H.W. Wilson, 1991).

La hormiguita

Un día de primavera, muy temprano en la mañana, la hormiguita preparó un pan para llevárselo a su madrina. Salió de su casa con el pan y se puso a caminar.

pum   pum   pum   pum

    pum   pum   pum   pum

Pisó una gota de agua. La hormiguita no lo sabía, pero la gota se había hecho hielo.

    ¡Aiiiiiiiiiiiiiii!

La hormiguita se resbaló sobre el hielo.

    ¡PUM!

Cayó al suelo y se lastimó el pie, y el pan se cayó en la tierra. Ahora ya no tenia el pan que llevarle a su madrina. Se sentó en el camino a sobarse el pie.

En eso llegó el grillo

—¿Que pasó?—preguntó el grillo.

—Me resbalé sobre el hielo, y me lastimé el pie, y se me cayó el pan que le hice a mi madrina.—dijo la hormiguita.

—Eso—dijo el grillo—es culpa de la escarcha. La escarcha congeló la gota, la gota se hizo hielo, y el hielo te hizo resbalar. Ve y pídele justicia a la escarcha.

pum   pum   pum   pum

    pum   pum   pum   pum

La hormiguita fue en busca de la escarcha.

Y cuando encontró a la escarcha, le dijo—Pido justicia. Tú congelaste la gota, la gota se hizo hielo, el hielo me hizo resbalar y me lastimé el pie, y se me cayó el pan que le hice a mi madrina.—

—No, no, no fue mi culpa - dijo la escarcha— Hay alguien más poderoso que yo. El sol me derrite a mí. Ve y pídele justicia a él.—

La hormiguita fue en busca del sol.

pum   pum   pum   pum

    pum   pum   pum   pum

Y cuando encontró al sol, le dijo —Pido justicia. Tú derretiste la escarcha, la escarcha congeló la gota, la gota se hizo hielo, el hielo me hizo resbalar ye me lastimé el pie, y se me cayó el pan que le hice a mi madrina–.

—No, no, no fue mi culpa—dijo el sol—hay alguien más poderoso que yo. La nube me cubre. Ve y pídele justicia a la nube.

Así que la hormiguita fue en busca de la nube.

pum   pum   pum   pum

    pum   pum   pum   pum

Y cuando encontró a la nube, le dijo—Pido justicia. Tú cubriste al sol, el sol derritió la escarcha, la escarcha congeló la gota, la gota se hizo hielo, el hielo me hizo resbalar y me lastimé el pie, y se me cayó el pan que le hice a mi madrina.—

—No, no, no fue mi culpa —dijo la nube — Hay alguien más poderoso que yo. El viento me arrastra. Ve y pídela justicia al viento

Así que la hormiguita fue en busca del viento.

pum   pum   pum   pum

    pum   pum   pum   pum

Y cuando encontró al viento, le dijo — Pido justicia — Tú arrastraste a la nube, la nube cubrió al sol, el sol derritió la escarcha, la escarcha congeló la gota, la gota se hizo hielo, el hielo me hizo resbalar, y me lastimé el pie, y se me cayó el pan que le hice a mi madrina.—

—No, no no fue mi culpa —dijo el viento — Hay alguien más poderoso que yo. La pared no me deja pasar. Ve y pídele justicia a la pared.

Así que la hormiguita fue en busca de la pared.

pum   pum   pum   pum

   pum   pum   pum   pum

Y cuando encontró a la pared, le dijo —Pido justicia. Tú no dejas al viento pasar, el viento arrrastró a la nube, la nube cubrió al sol, el sol derritió la escarcha, la escarcha congeló la gota, la gota se hizo hielo, el hielo me hizo resbalar y me lastimé el pie, y se me cayo el pan que le hice a mi madrina.

—No, no, no fue mi culpa — dijo la pared — Hay alguien más poderoso que yo. El comején me está comiendo. Ve y pídele justicia al comején.

Así que la hormiguita fue en busca del comején.

pum   pum   pum   pum

   pum   pum   pum   pum

Y cuando encontró al comején, le dijo — Pido justicia. Tú te comes la pared, la pared no dejó

al viento pasar, el viento arrastró a la nube, la nube cubrió al sol, el sol derritió la escarcha, la escarcha congeló la gota, la gota se hizo hielo, el hielo me hizo resbalar y me lastimé el pie, y se me cayó el pan que le hice a mi madrina.

—No, no, no fue mi culpa — dijo el comején — Hay alguien más poderoso que yo. El oso hormiguero saca su larga y pegajosa lengua para comerme. Ve y pídele justicia a él.

Así que fue en busca del oso hormiguero.

pum   pum   ¡**Ay No!**

   pum   pum

La hormiguita se acordó que su madre le había advertido del oso hormiguero!

Mejor no le pido justicia al oso hormiguero - se dijo la hormiguita a sí misma — En vez, se amarró una venda alrededor del pie, le sacudió el polvo al pan y se encaminó hacia la casa de su madrina.

pum   pum   pum   pum

   pum   pum   pum   pum

Nunca recibió justicia. Pero, por lo menos, no se la comieron!

Translated by Adela Artola Allen

sun

bread

drop of water

ant

cloud

wall

termite

wind

cricket

frost

Teeny-Tiny (England)

For sheer listening delight, few tellable stories can equal "Teeny-Tiny," an English *jump* tale (the final words are said suddenly as the storyteller jumps toward the audience.) It is a perfect story for the novice storyteller, for it almost never fails to delight an audience through its unique mix of frightening plot and ridiculous verbal style. Children will almost always ask to hear this story again immediately, and older children and adults appreciate it as much as the young children.

━━━━━━━━━━━━━━━━

Once upon a time there was a teeny-tiny woman who lived in a teeny-tiny house in a teeny-tiny village. Now, one day this teeny-tiny woman put on her teeny-tiny bonnet, and went out of her teeny-tiny house to take a teeny-tiny walk. And when this teeny-tiny woman had gone a teeny-tiny way she came to a teeny-tiny gate; so the teeny-tiny woman opened the teeny-tiny gate, and went into a teeny-tiny churchyard. And when this teeny-tiny woman had got into the teeny-tiny church-yard, she saw a teeny-tiny bone on a teeny-tiny grave, and the teeny-tiny woman said to her teeny-tiny self, "This teeny-tiny bone will make me some teeny-tiny soup for my teeny-tiny supper." So the teeny-tiny woman put the teeny-tiny bone into her teeny-tiny pocket, and went home to her teeny-tiny house.

Now when the teeny-tiny woman got home to her teeny-tiny house she was a teeny-tiny bit tired; so she went up her teeny-tiny stairs to her teeny-tiny bed, and put the teeny-tiny bone into a teeny-tiny cupboard. And when this teeny-tiny woman had been asleep a teeny-tiny time, she was awakened by a teeny-tiny voice from the teeny-tiny cupboard, which said:

Give me my bone!

And this teeny-tiny woman was a teeny-tiny frightened, so she hid her teeny-tiny head under the teeny-tiny covers and went to sleep again. And when she had been to sleep again a teeny-tiny time, the teeny-tiny voice again cried out from the teeny-tiny cupboard a teeny-tiny bit louder,

Give me my bone!

This made the teeny-tiny woman a teeny-tiny more frightened, so she hid her teeny-tiny head a teeny-tiny further under the teeny-tiny covers. And when the teeny-tiny woman had been to sleep again a teeny-tiny time, the teeny-tiny voice from the teeny-tiny cupboard said again a teeny-tiny louder,

Give me my bone!

And the teeny-tiny woman was a teeny-tiny bit more frightened, but she put her teeny-tiny head out of the teeny-tiny covers, and said in her loudest teeny-tiny voice,

Take it!

FLANNEL BOARD STORYTELLING

Make the house from a single piece of colored felt, cutting away the areas that represent rooms. The teeny-tiny woman's bed, blanket, and bonnet should be made of felt (for maximum adherence), and the woman herself, cupboard with candle, gate, gravestone, and bone should be of interfacing (so that you can draw details onto them).

Assemble the house and figures on the flannel board before beginning the story, the house toward the left-hand side. Place the cover on the bed. The teeny-tiny woman stands between the bed and the cupboard, and the bonnet sits on the cupboard next to the candle. The gate and the gravestone (with the bone on top) should be to the far right of the flannel board. Dress the woman and move her down the stairs, out of the house, and into the graveyard as you tell the story. When she returns from the graveyard with the bone, place the bone inside the cupboard, and her bonnet on top. Place the teeny-tiny woman in bed, under the covers. Move the covers up over her head, then pull them down again when she says, "Take it!"—and quickly remove the bone.

PARTICIPATION

Save participation for a second telling, in which children can begin to join in telling the entire story with you, using visual cues from your manipulation of the flannel board figures. Children can make their own small flannel board versions of "Teeny-Tiny," using the instructions on page 8, "Children Tell Stories with Flannel Boards."

LEADING TO READING

This story can be found in picture book editions illustrated by Tomie dePaola (Putnam, 1986), Paul Galdone (Clarion, 1984), and Barbara Seuling (Viking, 1976). Ask the children to compare the illustrations. Which are the most frightening?

cover

bed

cut
out

cupboard

bone

bonnet

gravestone

gate

teeny-tiny woman

The Hungry Cat (Norway)

This cumulative folktale from Norway is a variant of a widely known tale type found in the United States, Europe, and Asia, in which a hungry creature eats an impossibly large number of impossibly large objects, then bursts. It should be told so that it seems the cat bursts only moments before the storyteller's memory—and the audience's patience!—gives out.

Once upon a time a man had a cat that was so large and fat, and such a beast to feed, he couldn't afford to keep her any longer. So, he decided to take her down to the river with a stout stone about her neck. But before that, the good woman gave her a last meal—a bowl of porridge and a bit of fat.

The cat ate the porridge, and the fat, and after that, she went outside.

"Good day, pussycat," said the man. "Have you eaten anything today?"

"Oh, I've had a little bit to eat, but I'm still hungry," said the cat. "I ate a bowl of porridge, and a piece of fat, and I think I am going to eat you, **too!**"

And the cat gobbled up the man.

The good woman sat in the barn, milking Daisy the Cow.

"Good day, pussycat. Have you eaten anything today?"

"Oh, I've had a little bit to eat, but I'm still hungry," said the cat. "I ate a bowl of porridge, and a piece of fat, and the good man, and I think I am going to eat you, **too!**"

And the cat gobbled up the good woman. And Daisy the Cow.

The cat went outside, and there she saw Swishytail the Squirrel.

"Good day, pussycat. Have you eaten anything today?" asked the squirrel.

"Oh, I've had a little bit to eat, but I'm still hungry," said the cat. "I ate a bowl of porridge, and a piece of fat, and the good man, and the good woman, and Daisy the Cow, and I think I am going to eat you, **too!**"

And the cat gobbled up Swishytail the Squirrel.

The cat went along until she met Slyboots the Fox.

"Good day, Pussycat," said Slyboots the Fox. "Have you eaten anything today?"

"Oh, I've had a little bit to eat, but I'm still hungry," said the cat. "I ate a bowl of porridge, and a piece of fat, and the good man, and the good woman, and Daisy the Cow, and Swishytail the Squirrel, and I think I am going to eat you, **too!**"

And the cat gobbled up Slyboots the Fox.

The cat went along until she met Greedy Greylegs the Wolf.

"Good day, Pussycat," said Greedy Greylegs. "Have you eaten anything today?"

"Oh, I've had a little bit to eat, but I'm still

hungry," said the cat. "I ate a bowl of porridge, and a piece of fat, and the good man, and the good woman, and Daisy the Cow, and Swishytail the Squirrel, and Slyboots the Fox, and I think I am going to eat you, **too!**"

And the cat gobbled up Greedy Greylegs the Wolf.

The cat went along until she met a bridal procession upon the road—the bride and the bridegroom, and all the bridesmaids, parents, friends, and family.

"Good day, pussycat," said all the people in the bridal procession. "Have you eaten anything today?"

"Oh, I've had a little bit to eat, but I'm still hungry," said the cat. "I ate a bowl of porridge, and a piece of fat, and the good man, and the good woman, and Daisy the Cow, and Swishytail the Squirrel, and Slyboots the Fox, and Greedy Greylegs the Wolf, and I think I am going to eat you, **too!**"

And the cat gobbled up everyone in the bridal procession.

Then the cat went along until she met the moon.

"Good day, pussycat," said the moon. "Have you eaten anything today?"

"Oh, I've had a little bit to eat, but I'm still hungry," said the cat. "I ate a bowl of porridge, and a piece of fat, and the good man, and the good woman, and Daisy the Cow, and Swishytail the Squirrel, and Slyboots the Fox, and Greedy Greylegs the Wolf, and the bridal procession upon the road, and I think I am going to eat you, **too!**"

And the cat ate the moon.

Then the cat went along until she met the sun.

"Good day, pussycat," said the sun. "Have you eaten anything today?"

"Oh, I've had a little bit to eat, but I'm still hungry," said the cat. "I ate a bowl of porridge, and a piece of fat, and the good man, and the good woman, and Daisy the Cow, and Swishytail the Squirrel, and Slyboots the Fox, and Greedy Greylegs the Wolf, and the bridal procession upon the road, and the moon in the sky, and I think I am going to eat you, **too!**"

And the cat ate the sun.

Then the cat went far, and farther than far, till she came to a bridge, and on it she met a big billy goat.

"Good day, pussycat. Have you eaten anything today?" asked the billy goat.

"Oh, I've had a little bit to eat, but I'm still hungry," said the cat. "I ate a bowl of porridge, and a piece of fat, and the good man, and the good woman, and Daisy the Cow, and Swishytail the Squirrel, and Slyboots the Fox, and Greedy Greylegs the Wolf, and the bridal procession upon the road, and the moon in the sky, and the sun in the heavens, and I think I am going to eat you, **too!**"

"Oh, we'll have to fight about that," said the billy goat, and he put his head down, and butted the cat up in the air till she fell into the river, and there she burst.

Then, slowly, they all crept out, one after the other—the good man, the good woman, Daisy the Cow, Swishytail the Squirrel, Slyboots the Fox, Greedy Greylegs the Wolf, all the people in the bridal procession, the moon, and the sun. And they were all just as good as ever.

And as for the cat, not a trace of her was ever found.

FLANNEL BOARD STORYTELLING

Enlarge the drawing of the hungry cat so that it is three-quarters the width of your flannel board, and cut it from felt. Place the cat to the left side of the board; pin the tips of the tail and ears to the very top of the board. As the cat encounters each character in the story, place that figure to the right of the cat, then move it inside the giant creature, that is, put it on top of the cat's felt body. Practice placing the figures so that you will have room for all of them without overlapping any, if possible. After saying that the billy goat tossed the cat, causing her to burst open, remove the figures from the cat one by one, then flip her over the top of the board, out of sight of the audience, just before you say, "she was never seen again."

Figure 7. The hungry cat; smaller flannel board figures adhere to the cat, so that the audience can "see into" its stomach.

PARTICIPATION

Children will want to join you in reciting the ever-expanding who's who of the hungry cat's dinner menu. In a first telling, test the audience when the cat encounters the squirrel by pausing before each swallowed person or animal you name. Some children may begin to say the name of the person, thing, or animal being swallowed. If you wish to continue letting them guess in this way, pause for a beat before each item, then say the words yourself just a split second after the audience. You can also gesture toward the audience with an opened palm to signal that you want them to supply other phrases that are repeated verbatim, such as "Good day, pussycat."

LEADING TO READING

Similar tales of ravenous creatures are told in *The Clay Pot Boy*, a Russian folktale adapted by Cynthia Jameson (Coward, 1973), *The Fat Cat: A Danish Folk-Tale*, illustrated by Jack Kent (Parents, 1971), *The Greedy Old Fat Man*, an American folktale illustrated by Paul Galdone (Clarion, 1983), and a folktale from India, *Slip! Slop! Gobble!*, retold by Jeanne B. Hardendorff (Lippincott, 1970). Puppet patterns and script for an American variant, "The Hungry Monster," can be found in *Fantastic Theater: Puppets and Plays for Young Players and Young Audiences*, by Judy Sierra (H.W. Wilson, 1991).

man

sun

cat

woman

cow

squirrel

wolf

billy goat

moon

fox

bridal procession

See For Yourself (Tibet)

Although this particular folktale was collected in Tibet, it is known elsewhere in Asia, and appears in the *Panchatantra*, a story collection from fifth-century India. The chain of events in the tale is much like that in the English "Henny Penny" ("The sky is falling! The sky is falling!"). Though the moral of the two tales is very similar, the fleeing animals in "See for Yourself" not only learn their lesson, but also survive to profit by it. Children quickly realize the silliness of the hare's mistake, and laugh at all the animals running from the frightening "KERPLUNK!"

Long, long ago, by the shores of a calm, still lake there lived a timid little hare. Next to the lake grew a tall tree that bore one large fruit every autumn. And every autumn, the fruit would make a loud splash as it fell into the waters of the lake. But the little hare had only been born that spring. So when the fruit fell into the lake with a loud

KERPLUNK!

the hare ran away as fast as he could, shouting,

Run, run, run for your life.
KERPLUNK is coming after us!

A fox saw the hare, and heard what he said. So the fox ran along, too, crying,

Run, run, run for your life.
KERPLUNK is coming after us!

A monkey in the treetops heard them, and he ran along too, crying,

Run, run, run for your life.
KERPLUNK is coming after us!

A fat pig, wallowing in the mud, heard them, and he ran along too, crying,

Run, run, run for your life.
KERPLUNK is coming after us!

A great water buffalo heard them, and he ran along too, crying,

Run, run, run for your life.
KERPLUNK is coming after us!

A rhinoceros heard them, and he ran along too, crying,

Run, run, run for your life.
KERPLUNK is coming after us!

An elephant heard them, and he ran along too, crying,

Run, run, run for your life.
KERPLUNK is coming after us!

As the animals ran through the forest, fleeing the indescribably frightening KERPLUNK, they made a terrible, thundering noise. The noise woke the lion, king of beasts.

"STOP!" the lion roared.

And they all stopped.

"What is the cause of all this commotion?" the lion asked.

"The horrible KERPLUNK is coming," said the elephant. "I heard about it from the rhinoceros."

"The buffalo told me," said the rhinoceros.

"I heard about it from the pig," said the buffalo.

"The monkey gave me the news," said the pig.

"It was the fox who told me," said the monkey.

"I heard about it from the hare," said the fox.

"And what and who and where is this horrible KERPLUNK?" the lion asked the hare.

At that very moment, another tree dropped its fruit into a lake next to them,

KERPLUNK

"There it is again," shouted the hare.

The animals understood what had happened, and they were ashamed. But the lion just laughed, and sent them all home, saying, "Next time, don't believe everything you hear. Make sure to see for yourself."

FLANNEL BOARD STORYTELLING

Make the lakes, tree trunks, leaves, and fruit of contrasting bright colors of felt. Glue the leafy section to the tree trunks with fabric glue. The animals can be made of interfacing or felt. Set the large lake at the lower left corner leaving enough room to its left for the entrance of the lion at the end of the story. Place the small lake in the upper right. Put the matching tree to the left side of each lake, and place the fruit on top of the leaves of the tree. At the appropriate time, move each fruit from the tree onto the lake.

As the story begins, the hare stands with his back to the tree that is beside the upper lake. Thus, he can only hear, and not see, the falling of the fruit. Move him in one motion, to the right edge of the large lake. The other animals collect in a stampeding herd behind the hare.

You can tell this tale as a cumulative story, also. Simply recite the entire list of animals who are fleeing the terrible "KERPLUNK" each time a new animal joins in.

PARTICIPATION

The audience can join in on the refrain,

> Run, run, run for your life.
> KERPLUNK is coming after us.

Repeat this refrain twice the first time it occurs in the story, signaling or asking the children to say it with you the second time. You can also involve the

Figure 8. Flannel board for See for Yourself

children by giving them a chance to guess the name of each new animal character after you place it on the flannel board.

LEADING TO READING

Younger children can compare this tale to the English "Henny Penny," available in many picture-book adaptations, including that of Paul Galdone (Seabury, 1968). Text and flannel board patterns for "Henny Penny" can be found in *The Flannel Board Storytelling Book*, by Judy Sierra (H.W. Wilson, 1987). Older children can examine two other fables that tell of warnings about a terrible beast, *The Boy Who Cried Wolf*, retold by Katherine Evans (Whitman, 1960), and *The Judge*, by Harve Zemach (Farrar, Straus, 1969).

fox

large tree

hare

large fruit

small lake

cut to here — — →
for the
large lake

rhinoceros

small tree
and fruit

elephant

water buffalo

monkey

lion

pig

The Great Tug-o-War
(United States: African-American)

The tale of a small trickster who arranges a tug-of-war between two larger, stronger animals is well known in African and African-American folktale tradition. Sometimes the trickster ties the rope to a tree trunk and pretends to be pulling against a much larger opponent. This variant from Louisiana is especially satisfying because Brother Rabbit foils the elephant and the whale's mean plan to bully all the weaker animals, and manages to make fools of them not just once, but twice.

One day, Brother Rabbit was walking by the shore of the sea, and he saw something that was so strange, he just had to watch and listen. An elephant and a whale were talking.

Brother Elephant said to Sister Whale, "Sister Whale, since you are the largest and strongest in the sea, and I am the largest and strongest on land, we can boss all the other animals around. Anyone who doesn't like that, we'll just stomp them, all right, sister?"

"Yes, brother," agreed the whale. "You take the land, and I'll take the sea, and between us, we'll boss everyone."

"They may be the biggest," said Brother Rabbit to himself, "but I am the smartest. I am going to fix them good."

So Brother Rabbit went to get a rope that was long and strong, and he also got his drum. He took one end of the rope, and he went and found the elephant.

"Sir! Brother Elephant! You who are so good and so strong. I wonder if you could do me a favor?"

The elephant always enjoyed hearing such fine compliments about himself, so he said, "Brother, what do you want? I am always ready to help my friends."

"Well," said the rabbit, "my cow is stuck in the mud down by the coast, and I have tried and tried, but I'm just not strong enough to pull her out. If you could just take this rope in your trunk, I could tie it to the cow and you could pull her out. When you hear me beat the drum, pull hard on the rope, and we'll soon have her out of that mud."

"That's all right," said the elephant. "I guarantee I'll pull the cow out." And the elephant took the rope with his trunk.

Then Brother Rabbit took the other end of the rope and ran toward the sea. He went up to the whale and paid her some of the same compliments, and asked her if she wouldn't help him free up his cow that was stuck in the woods in a bayou. So, Sister Whale took hold of the rope in her mouth.

"When I hear the drum beat, I'll pull," she promised.

"Yes," said Brother Rabbit. "Begin pulling gently, and then harder and harder."

Then he went off a ways from both the whale and the elephant, so they couldn't see him, and beat on his drum.

The elephant began to pull so hard that the rope was stretched to the breaking point. Whale, on her side, was pulling and pulling, but she was losing ground and being hoisted onto the land because she didn't have any ground to plant herself on. When she saw what was happening to her, she beat her tail furiously and plunged headlong toward the depths of the sea. Now the elephant found himself being dragged into the sea.

"What's going on?" Brother Elephant wondered. "That cow must be really scared!"

So he twisted the rope around his trunk, and planted his feet in the sandy beach, and pulled so hard, he pulled the whale out of the sea.

He was astonished to see that his friend, Sister Whale, was on the other end of the rope.

"What's this? I thought I was pulling Brother Rabbit's cow," he said.

"He told me the same thing," said the whale. "He must have been playing a trick on us."

"He'll pay for that," said the elephant. "If I ever catch him on land, I'll stomp him good."

"And if he comes near the sea, I'll get him," said the whale.

Brother Rabbit heard what they said, so he had to think of another plan, quick. In the woods,

he found the head and hide of a deer that some hunters had left behind. He pulled the skin onto his back, and walked past Brother Elephant.

"Poor little deer, how sickly you look," said the elephant.

"Oh, yes, I'm really suffering," the deer replied (that was really Brother Rabbit). "That Brother Rabbit worked an evil spell on me. Watch out, or he'll work a spell on you."

Now Brother Elephant was frightened.

"Little deer," he said, "tell Brother Rabbit that I am still his friend. When you see him, send my regards."

A little later, Brother Rabbit met Sister Whale down by the sea.

"Poor little deer, why are you limping so? You seem sick today."

"Oh yes, Brother Rabbit did this with his magic spell. Take care, Sister Whale, for that rabbit can put a spell on you, too."

The whale was frightened.

"Give Brother Rabbit my best regards when you see him. Tell him I am still his friend," said the whale.

No matter who is biggest, Brother Rabbit said, I'm still the strongest—when I use my head!

FLANNEL BOARD STORYTELLING

For this story, all three characters—Brother Rabbit, the whale, and the elephant—should be made of interfacing and colored on both sides, so that they can face either left or right on the board. The deer skin should be made of felt so that it will

adhere to the rabbit. A piece of fuzzy yarn, approximately as long as the flannel board is wide, serves well as Brother Rabbit's rope.

As the story begins, the whale is in the lower right corner, facing left, talking to the elephant. Brother Rabbit is toward the top center, eavesdropping. Then, the elephant is moved to the upper left corner of the flannel board, facing right. When he agrees to help Brother Rabbit pull his cow out of the mud, flip him over, so that he faces the edge of the flannel board, and place one end of the yarn on his trunk. Handle the yarn gently so it does not fall off the board. After the whale agrees to help pull Brother Rabbit's cow, flip her over so that she faces the edge of the board. That way, she and the elephant do not see each other as they pull on the rope. Do not move either figure during the tug-o-war. When the elephant has pulled the whale up onto the beach, show this by flipping over first the whale, then the elephant, so that they face each other. Quickly remove both Brother Rabbit and the rope. After the large beasts speak face to face, remove the whale and bring back Brother Rabbit, disguised as the sickly deer. After he tricks the elephant, remove the elephant and bring back the whale so that Brother Rabbit can trick her also.

PARTICIPATION

In a telling without the flannel board, use a drum, like Brother Rabbit does, as the children mime a tug-o-war. Pause after the words ". . . he went off a ways from both the whale and the elephant, so they couldn't see him, and beat on his drum." Divide the audience in half and designate one group as the elephant and the other as the whale. They will mime holding a rope and having a tug-o-war as you beat the drum. Walk to the elephant's side, saying, "the elephant pulled," then walk to the whale's side, saying, "the whale pulled," repeating as long as interest is sustained. Then, stop beating the drum and resume the story text where you left off. The children will probably keep miming until the end of the tug-o-war. At that time, signal to them that their part is over, saying, "You did a good job. Thank you."

LEADING TO READING

Priscilla Jacquith's *Bo Rabbit Smart for True* (Philomel, 1981) includes this tale and three others, all illustrated by Ed Young in an amusing, comic book style. You can make flannel board figures or puppets to tell the well-known story, "Brer Rabbit and the Tar Baby," using patterns and script found in *Fantastic Theater: Puppets and Plays for Young Players and Young Audiences*, by Judy Sierra (H.W. Wilson, 1991).

Two picture book variants of this tug-of-war story are, from South America, Giulio Maestro's *The Tortoise's Tug-of-War* (Bradbury, 1971), and from Africa, Letta Schutz's *The Extraordinary Tug-of-War* (Follett, 1968).

brother rabbit

deer skin

whale

elephant

The Knee-High Man
(United States: African-American)

The poor knee-high man only wants to get "sizeable," but his efforts are doomed to failure (he's past the growing age). The theme of this African-American tale—a foolish person or an animal unsuccessfully imitating others—is also found in many other cultural traditions. "It's best to be yourself," seems to be a widely understood piece of wisdom, delivered in this tale by the owl.

———

Down by the swamp there lived a knee-high man, and he wanted more than anything to be big instead of little. So he sat, and he sat, and he studied about how he could get sizeable. He thought and thought, and finally he decided to ask Mr. Horse just exactly what he had done to get so big.

So the knee-high man went to see Mr. Horse.

"Mr. Horse," said the knee-high man, "tell me what you did to get sizeable."

"Let's see, well, I ate a whole lot of corn, yes, and then I ran all around the pasture as fast as I could, and that must be how I did it."

So the knee-high man, he ate corn till he was nearly sick, then he ran around and around the pasture till he was completely worn out. But it wasn't any use. He wasn't a hair taller.

So he decided to go see Mr. Bull, and ask how he got to be so sizeable.

"Mr. Bull," said the knee-high man, "please tell me how you got to be as big as you are."

And Mr. Bull thought for a while.

"I ate a whole lot of grass," said Mr. Bull, "then, I bellowed and bellowed just as loud as I could."

So the knee-high man stuffed two big handfuls of grass into his mouth, and he chewed on it, and he chewed on it, but he could hardly swallow it. Then he bellowed, and he bellowed, and he bellowed, till some of the grass went up his nose, and his throat was sore and aching. But do you know? He didn't get any bigger at all.

He sat and he studied about how Mr. Horse and Mr. Bull hadn't helped him one bit, and he thought he just might ask Miz Hoot Owl for her advice.

"Miz Hoot Owl, do you know how I can get to be sizeable? Now don't say I should eat corn, or grass, or run around the pasture, or bellow as loud as I can, 'cause I already tried that."

"Tell me," said Miz Hoot Owl, "why do you want to be bigger than you are?"

The knee-high man thought for a while.

"I want to be bigger so that if I get into a fight, I can win it," he said.

"Did anybody ever pick a fight with you?" asked Miz Hoot Owl.

"Well . . . no . . ." said the knee-high man. "But I need to be bigger so I can see a long ways off."

"Don't you know how to climb a tree?" asked Miz Hoot Owl.

Yes, the knee-high man reckoned he did know how to climb a tree.

"It seems to me," said Miz Hoot Owl, "that you don't have any good reason to be bigger in the body. But you sure do have a good reason to be bigger in the **brain**! Go home, and study about **that**."

And he did.

FLANNEL BOARD STORYTELLING

Cut the tree from felt so that the owl and the knee-high man will adhere to it. Glue green leaf sections to a brown trunk, and mark the knothole on the trunk with a black marker. Place the tree at the left-hand side of the flannel board. At the beginning of the story, the knee-high man is positioned immediately to the right of the tree. Leave enough space to the right of the tree for the knee-high man to travel to see Mr. Horse and Mr. Bull. After each of the knee-high man's attempts to become sizeable, he returns to his exact original position next to the tree. The children will be able to compare his height to the knothole, and see that he has not grown. When Miz Hoot Owl asks the Knee-High Man if he knows how to climb a tree, place him on top of the branch to her right. Remove the Knee-High Man after Miz Hoot Owl tells him to go and study.

Use a nei-ei-ei-ing voice for Mr. Horse, a bellow-ow-ow-ing voice for Mr. Bull, and a hoo-oo-oo-ting voice for Miz Hoot Owl.

PARTICIPATION

In a telling without the flannel board, ask the children to join you in energetically miming the Knee-High Man's imitation of Mr. Horse (eating corn, running in place) and Mr. Bull (eating grass, bellowing).

The theme of the story, that a wise person knows the difference between what can and cannot be changed, may be beyond some young listeners, but they will know the Knee-High Man was being very foolish to imitate Mr. Horse and Mr. Bull. Ask them what they think the Knee-High Man did after he got Miz Hoot Owl's advice.

LEADING TO READING

Leo Lionni's *Fish Is Fish* (Pantheon, 1970), and Richard J. Margolis' *Wish Again, Big Bear* (Macmillan, 1972) are good picture book tales for group sharing that feature characters who want to be different than they are.

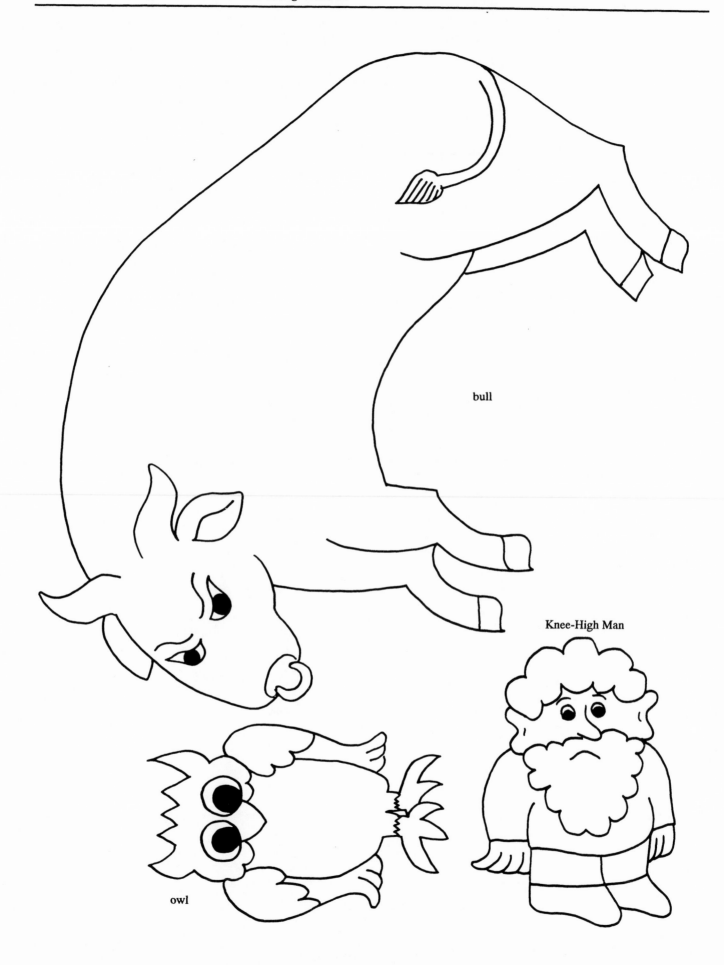

bull

Knee-High Man

owl

horse

tree

In a Dark, Dark Wood (Anglo-American)

This brief Anglo-American folktale is a perfect scary story for young children, because its slow rhythmic text and repetition make it obvious even to the youngest listeners that it could not possibly be real. It is also a good first story for children to learn to tell themselves. We often introduce this story by telling the children that they can learn it and share it with their family and friends.

In a dark, dark wood,

There was a dark, dark house,

And in that dark, dark house,

There was a dark, dark room,

And in that dark, dark room,

There was a dark, dark closet,

And in that dark, dark closet,

There was a dark, dark box,

And in that dark, dark box,

There was a **ghost!**

STORYTELLING

Beginning storytellers tend to tell this story too rapidly. Maintain a slow, suspenseful pace, pausing between lines, slowing more and more until you reach the end of the story. Adjust the loudness and abruptness of "a ghost!" to fit the age of the audience.

PARTICIPATION

If children are familiar with the story they will join in on the first telling. Be sure to tell the story at least a second time so that all the children can begin to tell it with you. On the third telling, ask them to act out the story as you tell it, making their whole body into first the woods, then the house, then the room, then the closet, then the box, and then the **ghost!**

LEADING TO READING

This and other short, scary—but not **too** scary—stories can be found in the beginning reader, *In a Dark, Dark Room, and Other Scary Stories*, by Alvin Schwartz (Marper, 1984). Other good sources of scary stories for young children are *The Thing at the Foot of the Bed*, by Maria Leach (World, 1959), and Joseph Jacobs' *English Fairy Tales* (Dover, 1967), and Margaret MacDonald's *When the Lights Go Out* (H.W. Wilson, 1988).

PART 3
Folktales for Children
Five to Seven

The Lion and the Mouse (Greece)

This story retells one of the fables of Aesop. Fables tend to lack the formula and repetition of folktales, and this one is no exception. Beginning with a tense and dangerous situation, "The Lion and the Mouse" ends in friendship and harmony. Its message, "little friends can be the best friends," is especially appealing to children.

It was a hot day, and the lion was sleeping in the shade. He was a big lion, sleek and elegant. As everyone knows, he was the king of the beasts.

Now, it so happened that a little mouse had lost her way. She ran here, and she ran there, and without looking where she was going, she ran right on top of the lion's nose.

The lion woke up! In a flash, he reached out with his paw, trapping the mouse underneath. The poor little mouse stuck her nose out from between the lion's toes.

"Oh, Your Majesty," she squeaked. "Please forgive me. I didn't mean to walk on Your Majesty's royal nose, really I didn't. Please, spare my life."

"Stop squeaking," the lion commanded, "and give me one good reason why I shouldn't crush you this very instant."

"Well," said the mouse, "we never know what the future holds. Perhaps one day I shall be useful to you."

"Ho, ho, ho!" laughed the lion. "What a joke."

The lion thought for a while.

"I guess it **could** happen that a mouse could help a lion. Goodby, little mouse, and be careful not to cross my nose again."

The mouse scampered away quickly.

A long time later, the lion was walking along, not looking where he was going, when he walked right into a trap some hunters had set for him. Down came a net and covered his body. He struggled, and he growled, and he roared, but he couldn't get free of the net.

Not far away, the little mouse was nibbling at some seeds.

"I've heard that voice before," she said, and she hurried over to where the lion lay in the net.

The little mouse chewed, and she chewed, and she chewed, and she chewed. Soon, she had made a hole big enough for the lion to escape.

"It was true after all," said the lion. "Little friends can be the best friends."

STORYTELLING

Heavily formulaic stories, such as "The Goat in the Chile Patch," have a structure that, once learned, can be easily expanded and improvised upon. Not so the literary fable, which is concise, and depends on exact wording and phrasing for its effect. "The Lion and the Mouse" must be learned pretty much word-for-word, otherwise you may find yourself telling a short and a rather dull plot summary.

Making Lion and Mouse Puppets

This story can easily be acted out using two puppets and one prop. Either use a commercially made lion puppet and a mouse finger puppet, or make your own instant puppets from a paper bag, an index card, and a rubber band, following the instructions given below. Afterwards, the children can make their own lion and mouse puppets, and tell the story to a friend.

Make the lion from a paper lunch bag, brown or white, with no printing on it. Smaller bags work best for young children. The lion's mane is made of yellow paper, five inches wide, and as long as the two short sides and one long side of the bottom of the bag. (See Figure 9.) Cut it into a fringe of strips one-half inch wide, stopping the cut a half inch from the long edge of the paper. The bottom of the bag will be the lion's face. Curl the strips around a pencil for a curly mane, and attach with glue across the top and two sides of the face. Cut eyes, nose, and teeth from colored paper and glue to the lion's face. Put your hand into the bag palm up, puppet face up, folding your fingers into the bottom of the bag. Lift and lower your fingers to make the puppet's mouth open and close. Cut two arms from paper and glue them to the sides of the puppet.

The mouse is just a round head on two legs, which are really fingers. Cut a two-and-a-half inch circle from an index card. Cut two round ears, and glue them onto the face. Draw eyes, nose, mouth, and whiskers with crayons or markers. Select a rubber band slightly shorter than the diameter of the circle, and staple across the back, edge to edge horizontally. Put two fingers down through this rubber band to form the mouse's legs.

Make the net from a twelve-by-eight inch rectangle of tissue or other lightweight paper. Fold the paper and make cuts from alternating sides as shown (Figure 9). Opened out, this net can cover the lion and easily be either lifted up or torn off by the mouse.

Figure 9. Lion paper-bag puppet, mouse finger puppet, and tissue-paper net.

Children as Storytellers

After the children each make a lion and mouse puppet as described above they can be coached through an activity in which each child acts out the entire story, using one puppet on each hand. As narrator, you can choose to either tell the entire story, or to pause at appropriate points to allow the children to improvise the characters' lines as best they can. When they are proficient at performing the story with their puppets to your narration ask them to pair off and take turns telling the story to each other, one child using puppets and narration to tell the story while the other listens.

LEADING TO READING

Share other stories of big and little friends: A tiny mouse proves to be a good and useful friend to a whale in William Steig's *Amos and Boris* (Farrar, Straus, 1971), and the two friends in Tomie dePaola's *Bill and Pete* (Putnam's, 1978) are a big crocodile and a little bird. Horton the elephant is a true friend to some microscopic creatures in Dr. Seuss's *Horton Hears a Who* (Random, 1954).

The Travels of a Fox (England)

In this English folktale, a fox sets out with a sack, and a bumblebee, and a deceitful request, "Will you watch my bag while I go to Squintum's? . . . Be careful not to open the bag." One thing is certain in folktales—if an order is given **not** to do something, it will surely be disobeyed. The repetitious structure of the tale encourages the children to predict what will happen each time the bag is opened.

A fox was digging behind a stump, and there he found a bumblebee. The fox put the bumblebee in a bag and he traveled.

The first house he came to, he knocked on the door, and he said to the mistress of the house,

"May I leave my bag here while I go to Squintum's?"

"Oh, yes," said the woman.

"Be careful not to open the bag," said the fox.

As soon as the fox was out of sight, the woman took a little peep in the bag and out flew the bumblebee, and her rooster caught him and ate him up.

After a while, the fox came back. He took up the bag, and he knew that his bumblebee was gone, and he said to the woman,

"Where is my bumblebee?"

And the woman said,

"I just peeped into the bag, and the bumblebee flew out, and the rooster ate him up."

"Very well," said the fox, "I must have the rooster, then."

So he caught the rooster and put him in his bag, and he traveled.

And the next house he came to he knocked at the door, and said to the mistress of the house,

"May I leave my bag here while I go to Squintum's?"

"Oh, yes," said the woman.

"Be careful not to open the bag," said the fox.

But as soon as the fox was out of sight, the woman just took a little peep into the bag, and the rooster flew out, and the pig caught him and ate him up.

After a while the fox came back, and he took up his bag, and he knew that the rooster was not in it, and he said to the woman,

"Where is my rooster?"

And the woman said,

"I just peeped inside the bag, and the rooster flew out, and the pig ate him."

"Very well," said the fox, "I must have the pig, then."

So he caught the pig and put him in his bag, and he traveled.

And the next house he came to he knocked at the door, and said to the mistress of the house,

"May I leave my bag here while I go to Squintum's?"

"Oh, yes," said the woman.

"Be careful not to open the bag," said the fox.

But as soon as the fox was out of sight, the woman just took a little peep into the bag, and the pig jumped out, and the ox ate him.

After a while, the fox came back. He took up his bag and he knew that the pig was gone, and he said to the woman,

"Where is my pig?"

And the woman said,

"I just peeped inside the bag, and the pig jumped out, and the ox ate him."

"Very well," said the fox, "I must have the ox."

So he caught the ox and put him in his bag, and he traveled.

And the next house he came to he knocked at the door, and said to the mistress of the house,

"May I leave my bag here while I go to Squintum's?"

"Oh, yes," said the woman.

"Be careful not to open the bag," said the fox.

But as soon as the fox was out of sight, the woman just took a little peep in the bag, and the ox got out, and the woman's little boy chased him away off over the fields.

After a while the fox came back. He took up his bag, and he knew that his ox was gone, and he said to the woman,

"Where is my ox?"

And the woman said,

"I just peeped inside, and the ox got out, and my little boy chased him away off over the fields."

"Very well," said the fox, "I must have the little boy, then."

So he caught the little boy and put him in his bag, and he traveled.

And the next house he came to he knocked at the door, and said to the mistress of the house,

"May I leave my bag here while I go to Squintum's?"

"Oh, yes," said the woman.

"Be careful not to open the bag," said the fox.

The woman was baking a cake, and her children were all asking her for some.

"Oh, dear mother, give me a piece," said one.

"Oh, dear sweet mother, give me a piece," said the others.

And the smell of the cake came to the little boy who was weeping and crying inside the bag, and he heard the children asking for cake and he said,

"Oh, dear sweet kind mother, give me a piece."

Then the woman opened the bag and took the little boy out, and she put the house dog in the bag in the little boy's place.

And the little boy stopped crying and had some cake with the others.

After a while the fox came back. He took up his bag and saw that it was tied fast, and he put it over his back and traveled far into the deep woods. Then he sat down and untied the bag, and if the little boy had been there in the bag things would have gone badly with him.

But the little boy was safe at the woman's house, and when the fox untied the bag, the house dog jumped out and ate him all up.

STORYTELLING WITH A PUPPET

Introduce the story by bringing out the fox puppet, and telling the children that the story is about a tricky fox who asks people to take care of his sack for him. Teach them the lines, "May I leave my bag here while I go to Squintum's?" and "Be careful not to open the bag," using a sly, foxy voice.

Have the puppet hold the bag with the arm that has your ring finger and little finger inside (grip the bag between your fingers and the palm of your hand). (See Figure 10.) Mime knocking on a door with the puppet hand that has your thumb inside. Move the fox's head up and down a bit as he says his lines. The children should be able to join in with minimal cuing from you—just a pause. When the fox leaves the bag at each house, drop it in your lap, and hide the puppet behind your back until the fox returns for his bag.

Fox Puppet

Draw a pattern like the one in Figure 10, using your hand as a model. The two smaller fingers bend forward and down when inside the puppet. They are shown stretched out to the side in the drawing since this is what the flat pattern will look like. Roll your hand from one side to the other while tracing it onto paper. Allow one-half inch all around for the seam. Cut two pieces of felt or other fairly thick fabric, soft or fuzzy. Stitch the two halves together, leaving the bottom open. Glue on felt eyes and nose. To make the ears stand up, cut them from good, thick felt, or from a colored sponge. Put the puppet on your hand, and bend your first two fingers down into the nose. The ears should be placed right on to the fold made by your knuckles. Glue the ears in place with contact cement (for sponge) or strong fabric glue such as Tacky or Sobo (for felt). Make the sack by cutting a nine- to twelve-inch circle of felt, and running a thread in long stitches one inch from the outer edge. Place dry beans inside the sack, then pull the thread and fasten it off securely.

Figure 10. Fox hand puppet

LEADING TO READING

This story is illustrated by Paul Galdone in the picture book *What's in Fox's Sack* (Clarion, 1982). Other tricky foxes can be found in the English folktales *Henny Penny*, illustrated by Paul Galdone (Seabury, 1968) and *Johnny Cake*, illustrated by William Stobbs (Viking, 1972). Read about real foxes to find out if they deserve the bad reputation they have in folktales.

Roly-Poly Rice Ball   (Japan)

"Roly-Poly Rice Ball" is a great favorite of children five to seven, who relish tales in which good triumphs over evil, and in which evil is firmly and fittingly punished. This is one of several Japanese folktales featuring rolling dumplings or rice balls that, when followed, lead to a magical realm. A brief cultural note helps children better understand this story. Rice balls can be made of sweet glutinous rice formed into a ball—sometimes rice balls are wrapped in a radish leaf or a sheet of nori seaweed. They are a good food to carry when traveling or hiking. In olden times, a Japanese man might carry the rice ball in a special pocket inside the bottom of his sleeve.

Once, two old men lived next door to each other. They were neighbors, but they could not have been more different the one from the other, for one was kind and generous, and the other was cruel and greedy. The one old man was so mean, he would get up in the middle of the night and pick the blossoms off his neighbor's peach trees. Then, when the kind old man's trees did not bear fruit, his wicked neighbor would not share his own peaches with him.

One afternoon, the kind old man went for a walk in the woods, taking with him several rice balls as a snack. After he had walked a bit, he took one rice ball from his pocket. But just as he opened his mouth to take a big bite, the rice ball slipped from his hand and dropped to the ground. It rolled ahead of him on the path, *koro, koro, koro, koro, koro*, until he could no longer see it. The old man looked here and there, on the path and among the trees, but he could not find his rice ball anywhere. Then he heard a small voice singing,

> Rice ball, rice ball,
> Roly-poly rice ball.
> Rice ball, rice ball,
> One roly-poly rice ball.

The man reached in his pocket, took out another rice ball, and let it drop to the ground. It rolled away, *koro, koro, koro, koro, koro*, and disappeared like the first. Soon, the old man heard that little voice again,

> Rice ball, rice ball,
> Roly-poly rice ball.
> Rice ball, rice ball,
> Two roly-poly rice balls.

The old man followed the sound of the little voice until he came to a mouse hole. As he bent down and peered into the hole, a small, whiskery nose appeared.

"Thank you for the delicious rice balls," said a tiny mouse.

"You are welcome to them," answered the old man.

"Because you have been so good as to share your food with me," said the mouse, "I have a gift for you." She pushed two boxes out of the mouse hole, one large and one small. "Which one do you choose," she asked.

Now, the old man did not wish to be greedy, so he chose the smaller box. Then he hurried home to show it to his wife. The two opened the box, and when they lifted the lid, out came the most wonderful things—fruits and candies and cloth and jewels and coins of gold and silver.

It wasn't long before their greedy neighbor heard about the kind old man's good fortune, and he came visiting.

"I hear that you have found some kind of magic box," said the greedy man.

"That is right," said the kind old man, and he showed his neighbor the treasures that had come from the box.

"How, exactly, did you happen to find this box?" asked the greedy neighbor.

The kind old man told him how he had walked along the path in the woods, and dropped the two rice balls, and how they had rolled into the mouse hole, and how the mouse had offered him his choice of two boxes. He was just about to tell how he had chosen the smaller of the two boxes . . . but his neighbor had already rushed out the door.

"Make me some rice balls, wife!" the greedy neighbor shouted when he got home. "But don't use the good rice. Use that old, rotten rice left over from last week. And hurry! I'm going to get a treasure box just like our neighbor's."

The greedy old man hurried along the forest path until he reached the place where his neighbor had dropped his rice ball. He took out one of his rice balls and let it fall to the ground. It rolled along, *koro, koro, koro, koro, koro*, until it disappeared from sight. The old

man listened, then he heard a little voice,

> Rice ball, rice ball,
> Grimy-slimy rice ball.
> Rice ball, rice ball,
> One grimy-slimy rice ball.

The old man ran toward the singing sound, and he dropped another rice ball. It rolled out of sight, *koro, koro, koro, koro, koro*, and again he heard the small voice,

> Rice ball, rice ball,
> Grimy-slimy rice ball,
> Rice ball, rice ball,
> Two grimy-slimy rice balls.

The man looked all around until finally he saw the mouse hole. He got down on his hands and knees and peered inside. Suddenly, the mouse poked her nose out and spoke to him. "Those rice balls were rotten," she said.

"They were good enough for a mouse," snapped the greedy man. "Now just give me my box of treasures."

The mouse pushed two boxes out of the hole, one large, the other small. "Which do you choose?" she asked.

The old man did not even answer, but quickly snatched the larger box and ran home with it as fast as he could.

"Wife, come here!" he cried. Together, their eyes wide with excitement, they lifted the lid of the box . . .

Out crawled ants and snakes and scorpions!

Out flew mosquitoes and wasps and bees!

The old man and the old woman began to run. The ants and snakes and scorpions crawled after them. The mosquitoes and wasps and bees flew after them. The old man and the old woman ran and ran and ran.

They may still be running, for all I know. But the kind old man and his wife lived long in peace and prosperity.

STORYTELLING WITH A PUPPET

Introduce the mouse puppet to the children before you begin telling the story, and teach them the first rhyme, "Rice ball, rice ball, roly-poly rice ball." Then hide the mouse puppet behind your back until she appears in the story.

Change the pitch of your voice when speaking the mouse's lines. When saying mouse's refrain the second time alter the tone of the delivery to communicate the mouse's disgust for the rotten rice balls. Children love the way the mouse changes the words to her rhyme, and her disgust with the spoiled rice, and the sound of the rice balls rolling down the path, "*koro, koro, koro, koro, koro.*" They often leave a storytelling session chanting "*koro, koro, koro, koro*" or "grimy-slimy rice ball."

Use origami boxes as storytelling props. Buy a package of origami paper that contains two sizes of paper, and follow the folding instructions in Figure 11 to make a large box and a small box, each with a lid. Set the boxes on a table beside you, close enough so that the mouse puppet can point to them and drop one on your lap when the man chooses it. Continue using the boxes as props, opening them at the proper moment in the story. After the storytelling, teach the children to make their own origami boxes. They can use origami paper—or typing or colored photocopy paper cut into squares.

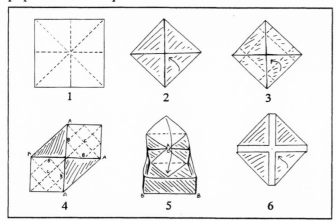

Figure 11. Origami box instructions.
----- Fold lines that have been opened out. **Step 1.** With colored side down, fold paper precisely in half diagonally, horizontally, and vertically. Open flat. **Step 2.** Bring each corner of the paper to the center point and crease along fold lines. **Step 3.** Bring the center point of each side to the center point of the paper. Crease along fold lines. Open flat. **Step 4.** Fold the two opposite corners to the center point. Lift the diagonal fold lines AB upward, bringing points B to C. **Step 5.** Repeat on other side. This will lift up the sides of the box. All four points of the paper meet at the center of the box. **Step 6.** To make lid, substitute step 6 for step 2. Bring corners to within 1/8–1/2 inch of center point, depending on the size of the box.

Mouse Puppet

Draw a pattern like the one in Figure 12, using your hand as a model. The two smaller fingers bend forward and down when inside the puppet. They are shown stretched out to the side in the drawing since this is what the flat pattern will look like. Roll your hand from one side to the other while tracing it onto the paper. Allow one-half inch all around for the seam. Cut two pieces of felt or other fairly thick fabric, soft or fuzzy. Stitch the two halves together, leaving the bottom open. To make the mouse's ears stand up, cut them from thick felt, or from a colored sponge. Put the puppet on your hand, and bend your first two fingers down into the nose. The ears should be placed right on top of the fold made by your knuckles. Glue the ears in place with contact cement (for sponge) or strong fabric glue such as Tacky or Sobo (for felt). Glue on a long, thin felt tail, and cut and glue on felt eyes, nose, and whiskers.

Figure 12. Mouse hand puppet.

LEADING TO READING

Rolling dumplings lead to underground adventures in two picture book retellings of Japanese folktales: *The Dumplings and the Demons,* by Claus Stamm (Viking, 1964), and *The Funny Little Woman*, by Arlene Mosel (Dutton, 1972).

The Wonderful Pot (Denmark)

"What's so wonderful about a pot?" the children ask when they hear the name of this Danish folktale. But the little iron pot on three legs has a mind of its own, a strong sense of justice, and it knows how to skip. Children's faces light up when the pot sits on the windowsill as the rich man counts his money. They gleefully predict what is about to happen. After listening to the story children commonly say, "I liked the way things switched. The rich man became poor and the poor man rich." And, "Do you think the pot is still skipping today?"

———

Once upon a time, a man and a woman lived together in a small cottage. They were very poor, and often they had to go without even a piece of bread to eat. In the same village lived the man's brother, who was very rich. He had a great farm with more cattle than you could count, and grain fields stretching as far as the eye could see. But he would never share anything with his poor brother.

At last, the poor man and his wife had sold everything they owned except one cow, and the day came when the man had to take her away to market. As he walked along the road, a stranger approached, asking if he wanted to sell the cow, and how much he would take for her.

"I think that twenty dollars would be a fair price," the man said.

"Oh, I cannot give you money," said the stranger, "but I have something that is worth much more than twenty dollars. Here is a pot that I am willing to trade for your cow."

Saying this, he pulled forth an iron pot with three legs and a handle.

"A pot!" exclaimed the man with the cow. "What use would that be when we have no food to put in it? My wife and children can't eat an iron pot. No! Money is what I must have."

The two men stood silent a moment looking at each other, when suddenly the three-legged pot began to speak.

"Just take me!" it said.

When the poor man heard this, he thought that if it could speak, it could probably do other magical things as well. So he closed the bargain, took the pot, and returned home with it.

Well, when he showed the pot to his wife, she scolded him, and called him a blockhead.

"Wash me! Clean me! Put me on the fire!" the pot cried out.

The woman opened her eyes in astonishment. Now she thought better of that pot, too. She cleaned and washed it carefully, and put it on the fire.

"I skip! I skip!" cried the pot.

"How far do you skip?" asked the woman.

"To the rich man's house! To the rich man's house!" And it ran out the door, across the yard, and up the road, as fast as those three short legs would carry it.

The rich man's wife was baking when the pot

came running in and jumped on the table. It stood very still.

"Ah," the woman exclaimed. "Isn't this wonderful! I need you for a pudding that must be baked at once." And she heaped a great many good things into the pot—flour, sugar, butter, raisins, almonds, and spices. She put the pot on the fire, but when the pudding was done, tap, tap, tap, went the three short legs, and the pot ran out the door.

"Where are you going?" cried the rich man's wife.

"To the poor man's house! To the poor man's house!" the pot called back to her.

When the poor people saw the pot coming back, and found the pudding, they rejoiced, and ate a wonderful meal.

The next morning, the pot again cried out, "Wash me! Clean me! Put me on the fire!"

The woman did so.

Then the pot said, "I skip! I skip!"

"How far do you skip," asked the woman.

"To the rich man's house! To the rich man's house!" said the pot.

Tap, tap, tap, went the three short legs.

The pot skipped to the rich man's barn. There, the workers were threshing wheat.

"Look at that little pot!" cried the man. "Let's see how much wheat it will hold."

They put bushel after bushel of wheat into the pot, but it just didn't seem to get full. Finally, when they had put every last grain of wheat into the pot, tap, tap, tap, went the three short legs.

"Stop! Stop!" called the men. "Where are you going with our wheat?"

"To the poor man's house! To the poor man's house!" the pot answered, leaving the men far behind.

The poor people were delighted, for that wheat would make them bread for the next year!

On the third morning, the pot once again cried, "Wash me! Clean me! Put me on the fire!"

And the woman did so.

Then the pot said, "I skip! I skip!"

"How far do you skip?" asked the woman.

"To the rich man's house! To the rich man's house!" was the pot's reply.

It was a bright and sunny day, and the rich man was counting his gold on a table near an open window. The pot hopped in through the window and sat on the table. The man continued counting his money and, although he couldn't imagine where the black pot had come from, he thought it would make a good place to keep his gold. So he threw in handful after handful, until all of his gold coins were inside the pot.

Tap, tap, tap. The pot ran across the table and jumped down from the windowsill.

"Wait!" shouted the rich man. "Where do you go with all my money?"

"To the poor man's house! To the poor man's house!" replied the pot, skipping down the road with the money dancing inside it.

The pot tumbled across the floor of the poor man's house, spilling gold coins everywhere.

The next morning, the pot said once again, "Wash me! Clean me! Put me on the fire!"

And they did so.

Then the pot said, "I skip! I skip!"

"How far do you skip?" they asked.

"To the rich man's house! To the rich man's house!" it replied.

Tap, tap, tap, it ran on its three short legs, never stopping until it reached the rich man's kitchen. As soon as the rich man saw it, he cried out,

"There is the pot that carried off our pudding, our wheat, and all our money!"

He threw himself on the pot.

Then he found he was stuck there.

"I skip! I skip!" cried the pot.

"Skip to the North Pole, if you wish," yelled the rich man, angrily, as he tried to get loose from the pot.

Tap, tap, tap, went the three short legs, and the pot ran out of the house, carrying him quickly down the road, and off toward the north, never stopping.

The poor people shared their new wealth with the other people of the village. They often remembered the wonderful pot with the three short legs that skipped so cheerfully. It was gone, though, and they have never seen it again since it carried the rich man toward the North Pole.

STORYTELLING

Creating a mental map of the small village in which this tale takes place—the road where the poor man meets the stranger, the poor man's house, the rich man's house and barn—and visualizing all the characters in place, will help you remember the story. The story is well designed to keep children in delighted suspense as they wait to see what sort of magic the pot can do, and what it will take the next time it visits the rich man.

PARTICIPATION

Encourage the children, through the use of a pause and expectant eye contact, to say the lines of the pot, "Wash me! Clean me! Put me on the fire!" "I skip! I skip!" etc., and to tap their feet on the floor to the pot's "tap, tap, tap."

LEADING TO READING

Read about other amazing pots in Tomie dePaola's *Strega Nona* (Prentice Hall, 1975) and Paul Galdone's *The Magic Porridge Pot* (Seabury, 1976).

Buchettino (Italy)

This Italian folktale tells of a small boy who tricks a large, frightening, and terminally stupid ogre. The advantages that children (small, quick, clever) have over adults (big, slow and oafish) are enchantingly played out in this story.

━━━━━━━━━━

Once upon a time there was a child whose name was Buchettino. One morning his mama called him and said, "Buchettino, will you do me a favor? Go and sweep the stairs."

Buchettino, who was very obedient, did not wait to be told a second time, but went at once to sweep the stairs. All at once he heard a noise, and after looking all around, he found a penny.

Then he said to himself, "What shall I do with this penny? I have half a mind to buy some dates . . . but no! for I should have to throw away the stones. I will buy some apples . . . no! I will not, for I should have to throw away the core. I will buy some nuts . . . but no, for I should have to throw away the shells! What shall I buy then? I will buy . . . I will buy . . . I will buy a pennyworth of figs."

So he did, and he went to eat them in a tree. While he was eating, the ogre passed by, and seeing Buchettino eating figs in the tree, the ogre said,

> Buchettino,
> Dear Buchettino,
> Give me a fig
> With your own little hand,
> If not, I will eat you!

Buchettino threw him one, but it fell in the dirt. Then the ogre repeated,

> Buchettino,
> Dear Buchettino,
> Give me a fig
> With your own little hand,
> If not, I will eat you!

Then Buchettino threw him another, which also fell in the dirt. The ogre said again,

> Buchettino,
> Dear Buchettino,
> Give me a fig
> With your own little hand,
> If not, I will eat you!

Poor Buchettino, who did not see the trick, and did not know that the ogre was doing everything to get him into his net and eat him up, what does he do? He leans down and gives him a fig with his little hand. The ogre, who wanted nothing better, seized him by the arm and popped him into his bag. Then he took him on his back and started for home, crying with all his lungs,

> Wife! Wife,
> Put the kettle on the fire,
> For I have caught Buchettino!

Wife! Wife!
Put the kettle on the fire,
For I have caught Buchettino!

When the ogre was near his house, he put the bag on the ground, and went off to do something else. Buchettino took out a knife that he kept in his pocket, and cut the bag open, and filled it with large stones, and ran away as fast as his legs would carry him.

When the ogre returned, he picked up the bag, and carried it home. "Tell me, my wife," he said, "have you put the kettle on the fire?"

"Yes," she said.

"Then," said the ogre, "we will cook Buchettino. Come here and help me."

And both of them took hold of the bag. They carried it to the hearth and were going to throw poor Buchettino into the kettle, but instead they found only the stones. The ogre was so angry that he bit his hands. He swore to find Buchettino and to bring him home for sure.

The next day, the ogre went all around the city and looked into all the places where he thought Buchettino might be hiding. Then, he heard a sound,

hee! hee! hee! hee! hee!

He looked up, and what did he see? Buchettino sat on a roof, pointing at the ogre and laughing so hard he had to hold his stomach to keep from bursting. The ogre's blood was boiling with rage, but he said in a sweet voice,

Oh Buchettino, please tell me,
How did you ever manage to climb up there?

Buchettino answered, "Do you really want to know? Then listen. I piled dishes upon dishes, cups upon cups, pans upon pans, and kettles upon kettles. Afterwards, I climbed up on them, and here I am."

"Ah, is that so?" said the ogre. "Wait a bit!"

And quickly the ogre took as many dishes, and cups, and pans, and kettles as he could find, and made a great mountain of them. Then he began to climb up, and up, and up, to catch Buchettino. But when he got to the top of the pile,

Tum,
Brututum,
Brututum,
Brututum, tum, tum.

Everything fell down, and the ogre on top, bruising his bones so badly that he limped off to his house, and you can be sure he had lost his appetite for Buchettino.

Then Buchettino ran home to his mama, who popped a piece of candy into his sweet little mouth.

STORYTELLING

Before telling "Buchettino," ask the children if they know what an ogre is. If not, we explain that an ogre is a mean, dangerous, monster-like person (make-believe, of course). Some children may compare an ogre to a troll. Children may not know what a fig is, though they've probably eaten fig cookies. Dried figs are sweet and chewy, and can be purchased at natural food stores, if you want to share some with your audience.

Use a gravelly or gruff voice for the ogre, and give a sing-song cadence to his lines. You can control children's reactions to the story through your portrayal of the ogre. Know your audience, and if you sense that some children may be frightened, portray the ogre as somewhat silly. When speaking for the ogre look upward as if looking at Buchettino in a tree. And look down, toward the ogre on the ground, when speaking for Buchettino.

Comments we have heard from children after telling "Buchettino" reveal how strongly they have identified with the hero. "I wouldn't tell the ogre how I got up!" a six-year-old girl blurted out the moment the story was over. Her peers said, "I would tell him the wrong way," and "I wouldn't give him the figs," and finally a ruse was suggested, "I would trick him and give him leaves."

PARTICIPATION

This story focuses children's attention completely, so it is best not to use participation until a second telling. A second telling (and even a third or fourth), with participation, helps children overcome any fear they have of the ogre. Invite them to join you on the ogre's lines, "Buchettino, Dear Buchettino . . ." and "Wife! Wife! Put the kettle on the fire. . . ." and on the sound of the ogre falling, "Tum, Brututum. . . ."

LEADING TO READING

Young readers can compare Buchettino to Tommy Grimes, a little boy who escapes from a cannibalistic neighbor in the picture book *Mr. Miacca* (an English folktale) adapted by Evaline Ness (Holt, 1967), and to the African girl Bimwili, in *Bimwili and the Zimwi*, retold by Verna Aardema (Dial, 1985), and of course to Jack in *Jack and the Beanstalk* (in Joseph Jacobs' *English Fairy Tales,* Dover, 1967).

Don't Let the Tiger Get You! (Korea)

The absurdity of objects such as a banana peel, an egg, a straw mat, and a rope walking into a woman's house and offering her their assistance counterbalances the terror of a midnight visit from a hungry tiger. This folktale was told to us by a nine-year-old girl, who learned it from her Korean-born mother. Similar tales of setting an intricate trap for a monster inside the house of the intended victim have been recorded throughout Asia.

Once upon a time, long ago, an old woman lived in a small house just at the edge of the forest. One day, she was tending the vegetables in her garden. She pulled the weeds that were growing around her carrots, and onions, and cabbages, and red hot peppers.

Suddenly, out from the shadows of the forest, there appeared a great, huge tiger.

"Ha! Old woman!" roared the tiger. "I will eat you up!"

"Oh dear me, dear me, dear me," the old woman wailed.

"Crying will not help you," growled the tiger. "I will still eat you up."

The old woman thought quickly.

"Oh, Mr. Tiger, you do not understand why I am crying. I am crying because I am so very thin that there will not be enough of me to make you a decent meal. Please, let me eat something, and fatten myself up, so that I may be a proper dinner for you."

The tiger licked his lips.

"Go home and eat, old woman. Tonight at midnight I will come and eat you up."

The old woman went inside her house as quickly as she could. She cooked up a big batch of onions, and carrots, and cabbage, and hot, hot peppers, then she sat down at the kitchen table and ate. Huge tears rolled down her cheeks as she tried to think of a plan to escape from the tiger.

A big yellow banana peel walked in the door.

"Why are you crying?" the banana peel asked her.

"Tonight, at midnight, the tiger is coming here to eat me up," said the old woman.

"Don't let the tiger get you," said the banana peel. "I'll just lie down here by the door, and maybe I can help."

An egg rolled in the door.

"Why are you crying?" the egg asked.

"Tonight, at midnight, the tiger is coming here to eat me up," answered the old woman.

"Don't let the tiger get you," said the egg. "I'll roll myself into the fire, and maybe I can help."

A straw mat hopped into the woman's house. "Why are you crying?" asked the mat.

"Oh, tonight, at midnight, the tiger is coming here to eat me up," answered the old woman.

"Don't let the tiger get you," said the straw mat. "I will lie on the floor in front of the fireplace, and maybe I can help."

In walked a rope. "Why are you crying?" the rope asked.

"Tonight, at midnight, the tiger is coming here to eat me up," said the old woman.

"Don't let the tiger get you," said the rope. I will lie on the floor next to the mat, and maybe I can help."

When the sun began to set, the old woman got into bed. The banana peel lay on the floor just inside the door. The egg sat in the fire. The straw mat lay in front of the fireplace, the rope beside it. The old woman trembled in her bed, waiting for midnight. Finally she heard the sound of the tiger's footsteps as he came closer, and closer, and closer. The door opened.

"I'm coming to get you!" growled the tiger.

"I'm coming! I'm . . .

Whooooooooaaaaaa!" The tiger slipped on the banana peel. He flew up into the air and landed in the ashes of the fire. . .

Blam! The egg exploded in his face. He jumped up into the air again. . .

Flammm! He landed on the middle of the straw mat, and he was knocked out cold. The mat rolled up tight around him.

Zippppp . . . the rope tied itself tightly around the straw mat.

The old woman received a large reward for capturing the tiger, and seventeen soldiers came and carried him away. Then the old woman sat at the kitchen table and ate carrots and onions and cabbage and red peppers. Huge tears rolled down her cheeks. That was because the peppers were so **hot** !

STORYTELLING

This story is easy to learn and tell if you create a mental map of the woman's house (think of it as just one room). If you find your mental map sprouting interesting images, use them in your telling, especially with six- to eight-year-olds. Once they are hooked by the suspense of the tiger coming, and become involved in trying to figure out how the woman's strange visitors will help trap the beast, children will enjoy added details that heighten their anticipation. They will let you know if it is taking **too** long. Use a deep, gruff voice for the tiger. The banana peel, egg, straw mat, and rope have very little to say, so this is an ideal story in which to try out some unique character voices, such as nasal for the banana peel, high and chirpy for the egg, low and monotone for the straw mat, and "sinuous" (rolling, up and down) for the rope.

Storytelling with Puppets

This story can be told with puppets and props, which can be made available to the children afterwards for their own retelling of the story. You will need two hand puppets, an old woman and a tiger. You can substitute another fierce animal or monster puppet for the tiger, but don't forget to change the title and words of the story accordingly. You will also need a banana peel (real, or cut from yellow felt), a plastic egg, a sushi mat or place mat that will roll easily around the tiger puppet, and a piece of thin rope, about two feet long.

You won't need a puppet stage, but you will need to tell the story next to a tabletop, on which you have set a bed and a fireplace made from shoe boxes and decorated with paint, colored paper, and cloth. Sit to the side of the table, and manipulate the puppets in front of you, just below your face. Move each puppet as it speaks, and hold it still, gaze focused on the other puppet as it listens. After the woman returns home, remove the tiger puppet and set it out of sight. Hold the banana peel, egg, mat, and rope, each in turn, and animate them as they walk and as they talk to the old woman. Place each of them on the tabletop, in its proper place relative to the furniture. Take off the old woman puppet and place her on the bed. Next, put on the tiger puppet and walk him through the trap. To make the egg explode, pick it up, say "POW," then quickly put it out of sight. Slip your hand out of the tiger puppet as you roll the mat around him, then tie the mat with the rope. Put the old woman puppet back on your hand as you finish telling the story.

Rehearse telling the story with the puppets several times. As you do so, you may find that acting the story out makes some of the narration unnecessary. It isn't essential that the puppets mime each and every action of the story. For example, it will look fine if you hold the old woman still as you describe how she fixed food for herself—or you can have her bend at the waist and mime various cooking motions with her arms.

Children as Storytellers

Have a group of children present the story as a puppet show while you narrate. Using the same puppets and props, they stand behind the table, in full view of the audience. Retell the story, pausing for the children to improvise words and movement.

LEADING TO READING

This tale is quite similar to *The Terrible Nung Gwama*, a Chinese folktale retold by Ed Young (Collins, World, 1978). Young readers can enjoy stories of children's narrow escapes from monsters in *The Gunniwolf*, by Wilhelmina Harper (Dutton, 1967), and in the beginning reader, *Wiley and the Hairy Man*, by Betsy Bang (Macmillan, 1976). These last two are adaptations of African-American folktales.

The Stonecutter (China)

This circular tale is so widely recorded in Asia, it would be difficult to attribute it to any one region. The magic of the stonecutter changing into anything he wishes appeals to children, though even the older ones may need to listen to the story more than once in order to understand how the series of transformations, always from a weaker into a stronger being, ends where it began.

A stonecutter was chipping away at the face of a mountain. Clink. Clink. Clink.

The sun was hot, and the stonecutter was tired.

"The life of a stonecutter is hard, and miserable," he said. "How I wish I were a great and powerful emperor!"

No sooner said than done—the stonecutter found himself transformed into an emperor. He was dressed from head to toe in silks and brocades, riding in a carriage of pure gold.

But wait. He was so hot inside all those clothes! The sun was beating down on him.

"So," said the stonecutter, "the life of an emperor is not much better than the life of a stonecutter.

> I wish,
> I wish,
> I wish to be more powerful . . .
> I wish to be the sun!"

In a flash, his wish was granted. He was the great sun in the heavens, the most powerful of all!

But wait. Something was covering him up. Something was more powerful even than the sun. It was a cloud!

> I wish,
> I wish,
> I wish to be more powerful . . .
> I wish to be the cloud!

In an instant, his wish was granted. He was a great billowing cloud in the sky, most powerful of all!

But wait. Something was making him move. Something was pushing him across the sky. Something was even more powerful than the cloud. It was the wind!

> I wish,
> I wish,
> I wish to be more powerful . . .
> I wish to be the wind!

And he became the wind. Joyfully he raced back and forth across the sky, and swooped down to the earth to bend the trees and stir up waves in the ocean!

But wait. Wham! Something made him stop. He couldn't move. Something was even more powerful than the wind. It was the mountain.

> I wish,
> I wish,
> I wish to be more powerful . . .
> I wish to be the mountain!

And he became the mountain—tall, old, and mighty. Nothing is more powerful than I, he thought.

But wait.

What was that noise?

It was the hammer of a stonecutter, chipping away at the mountain. The stonecutter was even more powerful than the mountain.

> I wish,
> I wish,
> I wish to be more powerful . . .
> I wish to be a stonecutter once again.

STORYTELLING

The use of wood blocks or clave to represent the "clink, clink, clink" of the stonecutter chipping and hammering at the mountain will underscore the cyclic nature of the story: make the sound at the appropriate point in the beginning of the story, then again, when the stonecutter has become the mountain (after the words "but wait"), to foreshadow his realization that the stonecutter is the most powerful of all.

PARTICIPATION

There are two ways children can participate in even the first telling of this story. The words "but wait" are always followed by a description of a more powerful object, which is not actually named until a complete clue is given by the storyteller. (You can elaborate on the clues, making them even more explicit for your listeners.) Pause deliberately before actually naming the object. Although few children may actually say what they think the object will be, their faces should indicate that they are actively engaged in predicting. Second, encourage the children to say the chant, "I wish, I wish, I wish, I was more powerful. I wish I was . . ." along with you. This offers them a chance to remember and say the name of the more powerful object, even if they may not have guessed it the first time, and gives them a feeling of accomplishment.

LEADING TO READING

A beautifully illustrated picture book rendition of this tale is Gerald McDermott's *The Stonecutter* (Viking, 1975). Compare "The Stonecutter" to other circular tales: the Japanese folktale, *The Beautiful Rat*, illustrated by Kaethe Zemach (Four Winds, 1979), and the folktale from India, *Once a Mouse*, illustrated by Marcia Brown (Scribner's, 1960).

Drakes-Tail (France)

This tale is based on a French variant of a tale type found in many parts of Europe. Stories of special friends with magic abilities appeal to a young child's vulnerability and need for protective companionship. "Drakes-Tail" is a long story, but the formulaic episodes, the repetition of rhymes, and, at the end, the life-threatening situations, hold young listeners' attention all the way through.

Drakes-Tail was little, but Drakes-Tail was smart. He knew how to save his money. He had many bags of gold, all hidden in a secret place.

One morning, the king went to visit Drakes-Tail.

"May I borrow some of your bags of gold?" the king asked.

"When will you pay me back?" Drakes-Tail wanted to know.

"Very soon, very soon," said the king.

Drakes-Tail loaned the king ten bags of gold, and the king took the gold to his palace. Drakes-Tail waited and waited. But the king did not come to pay him back. Drakes-Tail said,

> Quack, quack, quack,
> When will I get my money back?

And so he set off down the road to the king's palace.

On the way, he met his friend, Fox.

"Where are you going?" asked Fox.

"I am going to see the king, and to ask him for my ten bags of gold," said Drakes-Tail.

"May I come with you?" asked Fox.

"Yes," answered Drakes-Tail, "but the road is long, and you will soon grow tired. Make yourself very small, and hop into my mouth. I will carry you in my throat."

Fox made himself quite small. He hopped into Drakes-Tail's mouth, and sat down in his throat.

Drakes-Tail waddled on down the road, saying,

> Quack, quack, quack,
> When will I get my money back?

He met his friend Ladder, who was leaning against a wall.

"Where are you going?" asked Ladder.

"Why, I am going to see the king. I want the ten bags of gold he borrowed from me," said Drakes-Tail.

"May I come with you?" asked Ladder.

"Yes," said Drakes-Tail, "but how will you walk on your stiff ladder legs? Make yourself very small, and hop into my mouth. I will carry you in my throat."

So Ladder made herself quite small. She hopped into Drakes-Tail's mouth and sat down in his throat.

Drakes-Tail waddled on down the road, saying,

> Quack, quack, quack,
> When will I get my money back?

Drakes-Tail walked across a bridge. He looked down and saw his friend, River.

"Where are you going?" asked River.

"Why, I am going to see the king. I want to ask him for my ten bags of gold," said Drakes-Tail.

"May I come with you?" asked River.

"Yes," said Drakes-Tail, "but how will you walk on water legs? Make yourself very small and hop into my mouth. I will carry you in my throat."

So River made herself quite small. She hopped into Drakes-Tail's mouth and sat down in his throat.

Drakes-Tail waddled on down the road, saying

> Quack, quack, quack,
> When will I get my money back?

He saw his friend Beehive, hanging from a tree.

"Where are you going," buzzed Beehive.

"I am going to see the king, to ask him for the ten bags of gold he borrowed from me," said Drakes-Tail.

"May I come with you?" asked Beehive.

"Yes," said Drakes-Tail, "but how will you walk with no legs at all? Make yourself very small and hop into my mouth. I will carry you in my throat."

Beehive made himself quite small. He hopped into Drakes-Tail's mouth and sat down in his throat.

Drakes-Tail came to the king's palace. He knocked at the door and said,

> Quack, quack, quack,
> When will I get my money back?

The king was afraid. He had spent Drakes-Tail's ten bags of gold. He couldn't pay Drakes-Tail back.

"Throw this bird in the chicken coop!" he called to his soldiers.

The soldiers threw Drakes-Tail into the chicken coop. When the chickens saw Drakes-Tail, they said, "This is **not** a chicken! Peck him! Peck him!"

The chickens pecked and pecked at Drakes-Tail with their hard beaks. Then Drakes-Tail remembered his friend Fox, and he said,

> Fox, Fox, friend so true,
> Here is a chicken dinner for you!

Fox jumped out of Drakes-Tail's throat. He grew and grew. Fox grabbed as many chickens as his mouth could hold. Then, he dug a hole under the fence, and Drakes-Tail followed him out of the chicken coop.

Drakes-Tail went back to the palace. He knocked at the king's door and said,

> Quack, quack, quack,
> When will I get my money back?

"Throw this little quacker into the deepest well!" the king ordered his soldiers.

Down went poor Drakes-Tail into the cold, dark well. He flapped his wings, but he could not fly out. Then, he remembered his friend Ladder, and he said,

> Ladder, Ladder, friend so true,
> Drakes-Tail needs to climb on you!

Out came Ladder from Drakes-Tail's throat. Ladder grew and grew, and Drakes-Tail climbed Ladder out of the well.

He knocked on the king's door again, and said,

> Quack, quack, quack,
> When will I get my money back?

"Cook this bothersome bird for my supper!" said the king to his soldiers.

The soldiers put Drakes-Tail into the oven. Drakes-Tail got hotter, and hotter, and hotter. But then, he remembered his friend River, and he said,

> River, River, friend so true,
> Drakes-Tail needs to swim in you!

Out came River from Drakes-Tail's throat. River grew and grew. She put out the fire in the oven. Drakes-Tail swam in River all the way to the king's door. He knocked on the door and said,

Quack, quack, quack,
When will I get my money back?

The king opened the door. He told his soldiers to shoot Drakes-Tail. The soldiers ran aimed their guns at the little duck. But then, Drakes-Tail remembered his friend Beehive, and he said,

Grab —

Beehive, Beehive, friend so true,
Sting these liars black and blue!

soldiers

Out came Beehive from Drakes-Tail's throat. Beehive grew and grew. He let all his bees out. The bees aimed their stingers at the king and his soldiers. The king and his soldiers ran out of the room, out of the palace, and out of the kingdom. No one ever saw them again.

Drakes-Tail looked for his bags of gold. He looked in every corner of the palace, but he could not find them. That was because the king had spent them all. Drakes-Tail sat down on the king's throne. He covered his eyes with his wing.

When the people of the kingdom saw him sitting there, they said, "Wouldn't Drakes-Tail make a good king? He may be little, but he is very smart. And, he knows how to save his money."

So the people made Drakes-Tail their king. When anyone asks him how he became king, Drakes-Tail answers,

"All you need are a few true friends."

―――――――

STORYTELLING

Learn all the short rhymes of the story by heart, as well as the opening and closing paragraphs, and memorize the order of Drakes-Tail's four helpers and four punishments. This is a good story to "map" in your mind, seeing a bird's eye view of all the places Drakes-Tail goes. You may want to experiment with exaggerated character voices for the fox, ladder, river, and beehive, since each has only two short lines of dialogue, you won't need to worry about remembering the voices later in the story— have fun!

PARTICIPATION

Drakes-Tail's lament, "Quack, quack, quack, when will I get my money back?" is chanted many times throughout the story, and the audience will join in with just a little encouragement. Add gestures to the chant: when Drakes-Tail is on the road, hook thumbs under arms and flap elbows like wings;

later, when Drakes-Tail knocks on the king's door, point a finger angrily up toward the king. Encourage the audience to guess which one of Drakes-Tail's friends he will call on in each of his difficulties by pausing after the words, "Then Drakes-Tail remembered his friend . . ."

LEADING TO READING

Jan Wahl has illustrated a beginning reader, *Drakestail* (Greenwillow, 1978). Similar stories of unusual friends who march off to demand justice or reclaim stolen treasure are, from India, *Rum Pum Pum*, adapted by Maggie Duff (MacMillan, 1978), and from Vietnam, *Toad is the Uncle of Heaven*, retold by Jeanne M. Lee (Holt, 1986), and from Japan, *Momotaro, the Peach Boy*, retold and illustrated by Linda Shute (Lothrop, 1986).

Lazy Jack (England)

Jack, the hero of this English folktale, follows his mother's instructions to the letter, yet he's just too lazy to adapt old instructions to fit new situations. While laughing at Jack's foolish mistakes, listeners may fail to notice that by the end of the tale, Jack has become a hard worker and well paid to boot.

Once upon a time there was a boy whose name was Jack, and he lived with his mother. They were very poor, and the old woman got her living by spinning, but Jack was so lazy that he would do nothing but bask in the sun in the hot weather, and sit by the corner of the hearth in the winter-time. So they called him Lazy Jack.

His mother could not get him to do anything for her, and at last told him, one Monday, that if he did not begin to work for his keep, she would turn him out to get his living as he could.

This roused Jack, and he went out and hired himself for the next day to a neighboring farmer for a penny. But as he was coming home, never having had any money before, he dropped it passing over a brook.

"You foolish boy," said his mother, "you should have put it in your pocket."

"I'll do so next time," replied Jack.

On Wednesday, Jack went out again and hired himself to a cowkeeper, who gave him a jar of milk for his day's work. Jack took the jar and put it into the large pocket of his jacket, spilling it all, long before he got home.

"You silly fellow!" said the old woman. "You should have carried it on your head."

"I'll do so next time," said Jack.

So on Thursday, Jack hired himself again to a farmer, who agreed to give him a cream cheese for his services. In the evening Jack took the cheese, and went home with it on his head. By the time he got home the cheese was all melted and matted in his hair.

"You worthless lout," said his mother, "you should have carried it very carefully in your hands."

"I'll do so next time," replied Lazy Jack.

On Friday, Lazy Jack again went out, and hired himself to a baker, who would give him nothing for his work but a large tomcat. Jack took the cat, and began carrying it very carefully in his hands, but in a short time, the cat scratched him so hard that he let it go.

When he got home, his mother said to him, "You blockhead, you should have tied it with a string, and dragged it along after you."

"I'll do so next time," said Jack.

So on Saturday, Jack hired himself to a butcher, who rewarded him by the handsome present of a great roast beef. Jack took the beef, tied it to a string, and trailed it along after him in the dirt, so that by the time he had got home dogs had eaten everything but the bone.

His mother was this time quite out of patience with him, for the next day was Sunday, and she was obliged to do with cabbage for her dinner. "You ninny-hammer," said she to her son; "you should have carried it on your shoulder."

"I'll do so next time," replied Jack.

On the next Monday, Lazy Jack went once more, and hired himself to a cattle-keeper, who gave him a donkey for his trouble. Jack found it hard to hoist the donkey on his shoulders, but at last he did it, and began walking slowly home with his prize.

Now it happened that in the course of his journey there lived a rich man with his only daughter, a lovely girl who had never spoken a word in her life. Now this girl had never, ever laughed, and the doctors said she would never speak till somebody made her laugh. This young lady happened to be looking out of the window when Jack was passing with the donkey on his shoulders, with the legs sticking up in the air, and the sight was so comical and strange that she burst out into a great fit of laughter, and immediately recovered her speech and hearing. The rich man was overjoyed, and his daughter asked at once if she could marry Lazy Jack. They lived in a great house, and Jack's mother lived with them in happiness and contentment.

STORYTELLING

Memorize the story's basic time-frame: the day of the week, who Jack works for that day, what he receives, how he carries it, and what his mother calls him. Portray Jack's mother's building exasperation with her son, making her seem a bit silly in her anger.

PARTICIPATION

The second or third time Lazy Jack responds to his mother, "I'll do so next time," signal with an exaggerated nod of your head and pause for the children to join in. Also, pause each time Jack must decide how to carry the items he is given in exchange for his work. This will invite the children to remember how Jack's mother told him to carry it. If you wish, encourage children to join you in miming the way Jack carried each object.

LEADING TO READING

Two fine picture book versions of this tale are *Lazy Jack*, by Tony Ross (Dial, 1986) and *Obedient Jack*, by Paul Galdone (Watts, 1972). A modern literary figure who follows instructions to the letter, in a different but equally humorous way, is Amelia Bedelia, about whom Peggy Parish has written a series of books for beginning readers.

Why Do Monkeys Live in Trees?
(West Africa)

This folktale from the Ewe-speaking people of West Africa (parts of Ghana, Benin and Togo) is a humorous study in trickery and counter-trickery. It is one of many tales that claim to explain how animals who are now natural enemies were once friends, and how those friendships ended.

———————————

Long ago, the monkey and the bush cat were friends.

The bush cat went out hunting one day. All day long she hunted, but she didn't catch a thing. So she lay down and closed her eyes, but she couldn't seem to fall asleep. That was because so many fleas were biting her.

"Hey! Monkey!" cried the bush cat. "Come over here and catch these fleas so I can go to sleep."

The monkey came, and he caught the fleas that hopped in the bush cat's yellow fur, then he looked at the bush cat. The bush cat's eyes were closed. She was asleep.

"The bush cat looks so happy," said the monkey. "She looks so peaceful. I think I will tie her tail to this tree."

So he did. Then he climbed high up into the branches and waited.

The bush cat woke up and stretched. She wasn't tired any more, but she was still hungry. She wanted to hunt. But when she took a step, her tail pulled her back. The bush cat looked behind, and saw her tail tied in a big knot around that tree. The bush cat looked up, and saw the monkey laughing at her.

"Monkey! You come down here and untie my tail," roared the bush cat.

"Oh, no, you would catch me and eat me," the monkey cried.

A rabbit hopped by.

"Rabbit, come over here and untie my tail," the bush cat growled.

"Oh, no," said the rabbit. "You would catch me and eat me."

A snake glided past.

"Snake, come over here and untie my tail," the bush cat snarled.

"Oh, no," said the snake, "You would catch me and eat me."

The bush cat asked every animal she saw to untie her tail, but the only one who agreed to do it was the snail.

The snail took the end of the bush cat's tail in his mouth, and slowly—oh, so slowly—he untied the knot. It took him a long time. It took him two entire days to do it. And the bush cat spent every minute of those two days concocting a plan to make monkey pay for his trick.

The bush cat called together all her sisters and cousins and aunts, and all her other friends and relations, and she told them what the monkey had done.

"In five days, you are to have a funeral for me, yes, a big funeral with music and dancing. I will lie down and pretend to be dead. When the monkey comes to dance for me, and I will grab him, and eat him."

The animals did as the bush cat asked. They had a big funeral. The bush cat stretched out on the ground, and all the animals came. Some of the animals played the drum. Some of the animals danced. They danced in a circle around the bush cat, and they sang,

> The bush cat is dead!
> The bush cat is dead!
> Come dance, come dance!
> The bush cat is dead!

On the first day of the funeral, the monkey heard the drums. He wanted to dance, but he stayed safely in the tree.

On the second day of the funeral, the monkey heard the drums, and he danced all around the branches of the tree, but he didn't come down.

On the third day of the funeral, the monkey couldn't hold himself back any longer. He danced down from the tree, and he danced over to the circle of animals. He danced right up to the spot where the bush cat lay on the ground, silent and still.

The bush cat had her eyes open a little bit. She had her eyes open just enough to see the monkey, and she

> JUMPED,

and the monkey

> JUMPED,

and the bush cat

> RAN,

and the monkey

> RAN!

Faster,

and faster,

and FASTER!

Oh that monkey! He was quicker than the bush cat. He ran up into the branches of the tree.

He's still there. He knows that if he comes down, the bush cat will eat him up, because of that mean, mean trick he played.

Some days, though, when he's feeling sassy, the monkey hangs down from the tree branch by his tail and calls out to the bush cat,

"Help! Help! My tail is tied to the tree. Please come up and untie it for me."

The bush cat just snarls, rrrrrrrr.

And now you know why monkeys live in trees.

STORYTELLING

There are many good bits for the storyteller to dramatize in this story. Simple hand gestures enhance the children's image of small motions, such as the monkey catching the bush cat's fleas, and tying her tail to the tree. Facial expressions and body movements can help convey the reaction of bush cat when she discovers her tail is tied to the tree, and monkey's efforts to keep from dancing at the funeral. Speed up the pace of your telling, beginning at the point when the bush cat opens her eyes and JUMPS at the monkey.

PARTICIPATION

On a second telling, have a dance interlude in the story, during which you beat on a drum and the children chant, "The bush cat is dead . . ." and dance around in a circle. Use an agreed-upon signal to end the dance and send the children back to their seats.

LEADING TO READING

Other picture book tales of monkeys in trees are *Caps for Sale*, by Esphyr Slobodkina (Young Scott, 1947), *Fifty Red Night Caps*, by Inga Moore (Chronicle, 1988), and *The Monkey and the Crocodile*, a Jataka tale from India illustrated by Paul Galdone (Seabury, 1969).

The Cat's Purr by Ashley Bryant (Atheneum, 1985) tells a Caribbean story of how the cat and the rat became enemies; another friends-become-enemies tale is "Why Dogs Hate Cats," in *The Knee-High Man*, by Julius Lester (Dial, 1972).

Stone Soup (Belgium)

A soldier cheats the townspeople with his "magical" soup stone—or does he? When children ask themselves this question, and refuse to answer either yes or no, they have matured to a high level of moral development.

A soldier was returning home from the war. He had spent all of his pay, and his stomach was empty. He came to a village, and knocked at the door of a house and asked for something to eat.

"The crops have been poor," the woman of the house told him. "We don't even have any food for ourselves, let alone for strangers."

She closed the door.

The soldier went to another house, and another, and another, and at each door he heard the same story. It seemed that no one in the village had even so much as a moldy potato in the cupboard.

"These folks look plump enough," said the soldier to himself. "I might just have a trick to make the food dance out of their larders." He went up to the largest house in the village. He could have sworn that the smell of meat was drifting out the chimney.

"Good day," said the soldier to the woman who answered the door. "I don't suppose you have any food in the house."

"Not a crumb," the woman answered. As she began to shut the door in his face, the soldier took a step inside.

"Then it's a good thing I have come here this day. I've been abroad, at the wars, and I have acquired a magical soup stone."

"What a story!" said the woman.

"It's true," said the soldier, "and I'll prove it to you. Do you have a large pot?"

Yes, she had a pot. Soon, a fire had been built in the village square, and the pot set on the fire and filled with water. One by one, the people of the village came out of their houses and gathered around to see the work of the magical soup stone.

Then, with a flourish, the soldier produced a handkerchief from his pocket. Slowly he unwrapped the handkerchief, revealing what appeared to be a small, ordinary stone. The soldier dropped the stone into the water, and everyone stood around and stared into the pot.

And the soldier stirred the soup, and stirred the soup, and stirred the soup.

"You wouldn't have a bit of salt would you, to help it boil?" he asked. And a boy was sent at once to get salt.

They put the salt into the pot, and the soldier stirred the soup, and stirred the soup, and stirred the soup.

"The stone will make a tasty soup today, yes, just as it is. An onion and a carrot would improve its flavor, of course, but there is no use asking for what you haven't got," said the soldier.

Suddenly, a man remembered where he might just have an onion and a few carrots tucked away. They put the onion and the carrots into the pot, and the soldier stirred the soup, and stirred the soup, and stirred the soup.

The soldier tasted the soup. "It will be a fine soup. But a bit thin, I'm afraid, without a potato or two." A woman ran home, and came back with her apron filled with potatoes.

They put the potatoes into the pot, and the soldier stirred the soup, and stirred the soup, and stirred the soup.

"Some bones with a bit of meat left on them will make this dish fit for a king," declared the soldier. Several bones were suddenly remembered and brought forth. They put the bones into the pot, and the soldier stirred the soup, and stirred the soup, and stirred the soup.

Not only did the soup taste delicious, there was enough for the entire village, and the soldier as well. Everyone marveled at the wonderful stone that had made such good soup from just a plain pot of water.

"It's yours," said the soldier, "if only you'll promise always to share it, and to use it to make food for hungry strangers."

The people of the village agreed, and thanked him for giving up this treasure.

Fortunately, the soldier found another magical soup stone just before he reached the next village!

STORYTELLING

Just before you begin to tell this story, pretend to notice a stone on the floor, pick it up, wrap it in a cloth, and place it in an imaginary (or real) pocket. Later, take the stone out of your imaginary pocket "with a flourish," as the solider in the story does, and make an exaggerated gesture of dropping it into the pot. Accompany the refrain, "and the soldier stirred the pot, and stirred the pot, and stirred the pot" with a stirring motion that shows just how large that soup pot is. Mime the action of the soldier giving the stone to one of the people of the village, and seeing and picking up another stone on his further travels.

PARTICIPATION

Signal to the audience to join you in pretending to stir the soup, and to say the words, ". . . and the soldier stirred the soup, and stirred the soup, and stirred the soup." If you're having too much fun to end the story, keep adding more ingredients—take suggestions from the audience.

LEADING TO READING

Marcia Brown tells a similar version in *Stone Soup* (Scribner's 1947), while Tony Ross's picture book of the same name (Dial, 1987) is a surprising and funny modern version. *Nail Soup*, by Harve Zemach (Follett, 1964), is a variant in which a tramp cooks up soup for a woman using "only a nail."

PART 4
Resources for Storytelling

Resources for Storytelling

A dedicated storyteller is always looking for more good stories to tell. Telling a story is very personal, so a story must strike a responsive chord in the teller. As one librarian storyteller put it, "Stories seem to choose you!" A story really should inspire you to want to tell it; in fact, the desire to share a particular story is more important to a storyteller's success and satisfaction than any number of workshops or how-to manuals. The following bibliographies should help you find even more good multicultural folktales, as well as give you ideas on how to tell them.

I. FOLKTALES FOR PICTURE BOOK STORYTELLING

As most of us know from experience, not all picture books work equally well when shared with groups of children. Many picture book versions of stories from the folk tradition do not read well aloud. They may have far too much text for young children to listen to in a story hour situation, or the story adaptation may simply be poorly written. Illustrations may be too small or detailed for children to see and appreciate.

The illustrated folktales listed below have the special qualities which make a book suited for sharing with young audiences. These qualities are:

- Illustrations that can be appreciated from a distance of ten or fifteen feet. The youngest children need large, clearly defined characters and objects, set against a light or white background.
- Engaging and direct language that flows along, with rhythm and repetition.
- A small amount of text on each page. The story needs to proceed at a steady pace, with page turns revealing new illustrations, to keep a group's attention.

- Print that is large and clear enough to be scanned from a greater than normal distance (even upside down) by the story reader.

The authors listed below are, of course, adapters or retellers of traditional material. If no illustrator is specified, the author is also the illustrator. The country or area of origin is given as listed in the book.

Aardema, Verna. *Bimwili and the Zimwi*. Illus. by Susan Meddaugh. New York: Dial, 1985. (Zanzibar)

————. *Bringing the Rain to Kapiti Plain*. Illus. by Beatriz Vidal. New York: Dial, 1981. (Africa: Nandi)

————. *Why Mosquitos Buzz in People's Ears*. Illus. by Leo and Diane Dillon. Dial, 1975. (Africa)

Aruego, Jose and Aruego, Ariane. *A Crocodile's Tale*. New York: Scribner's, 1972. (Philippines)

Baker, Betty. *Rat Is Dead and Ant Is Sad*. Illus. by Mamoru Funai. New York: Harper, 1981. (Native American: Pueblo)

Bang, Betsy. *The Old Woman and the Red Pumpkin*. Illus. by Molly Garrett Bang. New York: Macmillan, 1975. (India)

————. *The Old Woman and the Rice Thief*. Illus. by Molly Garrett Bang. New York: Greenwillow, 1978. (India)

————. *Wiley and the Hairy Man*. Illus. by Molly Garrett Bang. New York: Macmillan, 1976. (United States)

Bennett, Jill. *Teeny Tiny*. Illus. by Tomie dePaola. New York: Putnam's, 1986. (England)

Blia Xiong. *Nine-in-One, Grrr! Grrr!* San Francisco, CA: Children's Book Press, 1989. (Southeast Asia: Hmong)

Demi. *Chen Ping and His Magic Axe.* New York: Dodd, 1987. (China)

dePaola, Tomie. *Fin M'Coul: The Giant of Knockmany Hill.* New York: Holiday, 1981. (Ireland)

———. *The Legend of Bluebonnet.* New York: Putnam, 1983. (Native American: Comanche)

Duff, Maggie. *Rum Pum Pum.* Illus. by Jose Aruego and Ariane Dewey. New York: Macmillan, 1978. (India)

Galdone, Joanna. *The Tailypo.* Illus. by Paul Galdone. New York: Seabury, 1977. (United States)

Galdone, Paul. *The Greedy Old Fat Man.* New York: Clarion, 1983. (United States)

———. *Henny-Penny.* New York: Seabury, 1968. (England)

———. *The Little Red Hen.* New York: Seabury, 1973. (England)

———. *Little Red Riding Hood.* New York: McGraw Hill, 1974. (France)

———. *The Monkey and the Crocodile.* New York: Seabury, 1969. (India)

———. *Obedient Jack.* New York: Seabury, 1972. (England)

———. *The Old Woman and Her Pig.* New York: Whittlesey, 1960. (England)

———. *Puss in Boots.* New York: Seabury, 1976. (France)

———. *The Teeny-Tiny Woman.* New York: Clarion, 1984. (England)

———. *The Three Bears.* New York: Seabury, 1972. (England)

———. *The Three Billy Goats Gruff.* New York: Seabury, 1973. (Norway)

———. *The Three Little Pigs.* New York: Ticknor & Fields, 1970. (England)

———. *The Three Sillies.* Boston: Houghton, 1981. (England)

———. *The Three Wishes.* New York: McGraw Hill, 1961. (England)

———. *What's in Fox's Sack?* New York: Clarion, 1982. (England)

Ginsburg, Mirra. *The Chinese Mirror.* Illus. by Margot Zemach. San Diego, CA: Harcourt Brace, 1988. (Korea)

———. *Mushroom in the Rain.* Illus. by Jose Aruego and Ariane Dewey. New York: MacMillan, 1974. (Russia)

Goble, Paul. *Iktomi and the Berries.* New York: Orchard, 1989. (Native American: Plains)

———. *Iktomi and the Boulder.* New York: Orchard, 1988. (Native American: Plains)

Grimm, Jakob and Grimm, Wilhelm. *The Shoemaker and the Elves.* Illus. by Paul Galdone. (Germany)

Haley, Gail E. *A Story! A Story!* New York: Atheneum, 1970. (Africa: Ashanti)

Harper, Wilhelmina. *The Gunniwolf.* Illus. by William Wiesner. New York: Dutton, 1967. (United States)

Hou-tien, Cheng. *Six Chinese Brothers.* New York: Holt, 1979. (China)

Jacobs, Joseph. *Munachar and Manachar.* Illus. by Anne Rockwell. New York: Crowell, 1970. (Ireland)

Jameson, Cynthia. *The Clay Pot Boy.* Illus. by Arnold Lobel. New York: Coward, 1973. (Soviet Union)

Kent, Jack. *The Fat Cat.* New York: Parents, 1971. (Denmark)

Lexau, Joan. *The Crocodile and the Hen.* Illus. by Joan Sandin. New York: Harper, 1969. (Congo)

McDermott, Gerald. *Anansi the Spider.* New York: Holt, 1972. (Africa: Ashanti)

———. *Arrow to the Sun*. Viking, 1974. (Native American: Pueblo)

———. *The Stone-Cutter*. New York: Viking, 1975. (Japan)

Maestro, Giulio. *The Tortoise's Tug of War*. Scarsdale, NY: Bradbury, 1971. (South America)

Matsui, Tadashi. *Oniroku and the Carpenter*. Illus. by Suekichi Akaba. Englewood Cliffs, NJ: Prentice Hall, 1963. (Japan)

Mosel, Arlene. *The Funny Little Woman*. Illus. by Blair Lent. New York: Dutton, 1972. (Japan)

———. *Tikki Tikki Tembo*. Illus. by Blair Lent. New York: Holt, 1968. (China)

Oxenbury, Helen. *The Great Big Enormous Turnip*. New York: Watts, 1968. (Soviet Union)

Ross, Tony. *Lazy Jack*. New York: Dial, 1986. (England)

Schutz, Letta. *The Extraordinary Tug-of-War*. Illus. by John Burningham. New York: Follett, 1968. (Nigeria)

Shibano, Tamizo. *The Old Man Who Made the Trees Bloom*. Illus. by Bunshu Iguchi. Union City, CA: Heaian, 1985. (Japan)

Sleator, William. *The Angry Moon*. Illus. by Blair Lent. Boston: Little, Brown, 1970. (Native American: Northwest Coast)

Tresselt, Alvin. *The Mitten*. Illus. by Yaroslava. New York: Lothrop, 1964. (Ukraine)

Wahl, Jan. *Drakestail*. New York: Greenwillow, 1978. (France)

Westwood, Jennifer. *Going to Squintum's*. Illus. by Fiona French. New York: Dial, 1985. (England)

Wiesner, William. *Turnabout*. New York: Seabury, 1972. (Norway)

Zemach, Margot. *The Three Little Pigs*. New York: Farrar, Straus, 1988. (England)

II. OTHER SOURCES OF FOLKTALES TO TELL TO YOUNG CHILDREN

Too often, those who rewrite folktales for young children fail to preserve the rhythm and repetition that hold children's attention; often they compound their mistake by "softening" parts of the stories that they fear are too suspenseful or frightening for children. Much of the satisfaction that children derive from folktales is a vicarious encounter with danger. While a child listening at bedtime may not complain about such adulterated tales, groups of children at storytime are not so polite—their interest soon wanders. Well-selected and well-told tales, such as those in the following collections, elicit responses of deep attention, spontaneous re-telling, and requests for the storyteller to "tell it again."

Jacobs, Joseph. *English Folk and Fairy Tales*. New York: Putnam, n.d. Dover Reprint [Title: English Fairy Tales], 1967.
Storytellers' number one choice for delightfully oral versions of such English classics as "The Three Pigs" and "Johnny Cake." Jacobs also edited other anthologies of English, Celtic, and East Indian tales.

MacDonald, Margaret Read. *Twenty Tellable Tales: Audience Participation Folktales for the Beginning Storyteller*. Bronx, NY: H.W. Wilson, 1986.
These twenty folktales from many cultures are retold by a master storyteller—simply, and with the ample repetition that young audiences adore.

———. *When the Lights Go Out: Twenty Scary Stories to Tell*. Bronx, NY: H.W. Wilson, 1988.
Twenty moderately gruesome tales–less frightening than most children want, and more gory than many overprotective storytellers are willing to give them. A good resource to use on the many occasions when children request something scary.

Pellowski, Anne. *The Story Vine: A Source Book of Unusual and Easy-to-Tell Stories from Around the World*. New York: Macmillan, 1984.
This book features some traditional ways to accompany stories, such as string figures, drawing, dolls, fingerplays, and simple musical instruments. Cultural background of the stories, and ample how-to illustrations are included.

Robinson, Adjai. *Singing Tales of Africa.* Illus. by Christine Price. New York: Scribner's, 1974.
These stories are memorable enough to learn quickly, and all include songs which are repeated in the course of the storytelling. Musical notation is provided.

Sierra, Judy. *The Flannel Board Storytelling Book.* Bronx, NY: H.W. Wilson, 1987.
Thirty-six songs, poems, and folktales in an easy, tellable format, each accompanied by traceable patterns for flannel board figures.

———. *Fantastic Theater: Puppets and Plays for Young Performers and Young Audiences.* Bronx, NY: H.W. Wilson, 1991.
This book contains scripts and puppet patterns for thirty plays based on folktales from many cultures, folk songs, and nursery rhymes. The patterns may be adapted for use as flannel board figures.

Tashjian, Virginia. *Juba This and Juba That: Story Hour Stretches for Large and Small Groups.* Boston: Little, Brown, 1969.

———. *With a Deep Sea Smile: Story Hour Stretches for Large and Small Groups.* Boston: Little, Brown, 1974.
Written with library story hours in mind, Tashjian's books contain attention-grabbing, participatory, often-silly stories, many from the folk tradition.

Withers, Carl. *I Saw a Rocket Walk a Mile: Nonsense Tales, Chants, and Songs from Many Lands.* New York, Holt, 1965.

———. *A World of Nonsense: Strange and Humorous Tales from Many Lands.* New York: Holt, 1968.
Withers' two collections include a world-wide variety of the humorous, repetitious, cumulative types of tales that young children love.

III. INDEXES AND BIBLIOGRAPHIC SOURCES

The following works will help you track down a tale in a collection, find similar tales from different cultures, and learn more about multicultural storytelling traditions.

Eastman, Mary Huse. *Index to Fairy Tales, Myths and Legends.* 2nd ed. Boston: Faxon, 1926.

———. *Index to Fairy Tales, Myths and Legends.* Supplement. Boston: F.W. Faxon, 1937.

———. *Index to Fairy Tales, Myths and Legends.* Second Supplement. Boston: F.W. Faxon, 1952.
Mary Huse Eastman's three indexes include folktales, fairy tales, myths and legends as they appear in collections published for children. Many of the stories indexed have been heavily rewritten to make them "suitable for children," and are quite dated. However, one finds in these early indexes the works of anthologist-retellers such as Joseph Jacobs, Seamus MacManus, and Parker Fillore that remain eminently tellable today. Indexing in these three volumes by Eastman is by title and alternative title only.

Ireland, Norma O. *Index to Fairy Tales 1949-1972: Including Folklore, Legends and Myths in Collections.* [Third Supplement]. Metuchen, NJ: Scarecrow, 1973.

———. *Index to Fairy Tales 1973-1977: Including Folklore, Legends and Myths in Collections.* Fourth Supplement. Metuchen, NJ: Scarecrow, 1985.

———, and Sprung, Joseph W. *Index to Fairy Tales 1978-1986: Including Folklore, Legends and Myths in Collections.* Fifth Supplement. Metuchen, NJ: Scarecrow, 1989.
Ireland, later in collaboration with Joseph Sprung, continues Eastman's work, adding useful access not only by title, but also by subject, area of origin, and major compilers and retellers.

Lipman, Doug. "In Quest of the Folk Tale." *Yarnspinner* 14:4 (June, 1990), pp. 1-3.
A brief and user-friendly guide for the intrepid folktale researcher with access to a university library.

MacDonald, Margaret Read. *The Storyteller's Sourcebook: A Subject, Title, and Motif Index to Folklore Collections for Children.* Detroit: Gale/Neal-Schuman, 1982.
MacDonald's work indexes folktales in collections as well as in single edition, which were in print between 1960-80. Multiple indexes provide access

to tales by title, names and types of characters, name of adapter, compiler and reteller, and geographic origin. In the main body of the work, tales are classified by "motif," a sort of combination of plot and theme. This organization brings together similar tales from different cultures, and makes this index a good starting point for researching stories cross-culturally.

Pellowski, Anne. *The World of Storytelling*. Bronx, NY: H.W. Wilson, 1990.

Those who choose to tell stories from cultures other than their own have a responsibility to learn as much about the stories and their natural habitat as possible. This encyclopedic work, nicely illustrated with photographs, provides an overview of world storytelling traditions, along with an excellent bibliography as a starting point for more in-depth research.

Index
by Linda Webster

JUDY SIERRA is assistant professor in the division of library and information science at San Jose State University. She is author or co-author of several books on storytelling and is a leader of storytelling workshops. Ms. Sierra received masters degrees in both librarianship and folklore and is currently a doctoral candidate in folklore.

ROBERT KAMINSKI, an active storyteller and puppeteer, has co-authored a previous book on storytelling with Judy Sierra. He is currently teaching English as a second language, and has extensive experience working as an artist in schools. Mr. Kaminski received his M.A. in theatre.

ADELA ARTOLA ALLEN is the associate dean of the Graduate College of the University of Arizona. She has taught classes in children's literature, bilingual reading, reading and writing, and language and culture. Her research interests are in the area of multi-ethnic children's literature, storytelling, and library services for Hispanic children. She has published extensively in this area.